THE UNSOLVABLE PROBLEM

PROLOGUE
UNLOCKING THE UNSOLVABLE MYSTERIES

In the vast expanse of human curiosity, the pursuit of knowledge has been an enduring and relentless quest, spanning millennia and transcending cultures. From the earliest civilizations, where philosophers and sages sought to unravel the mysteries of existence, to the modern era of scientific inquiry and technological advancement, the thirst for understanding has driven humanity to push the boundaries of the known.

Yet, as we delve deeper into the realms of science, mathematics, and philosophy, we encounter a profound paradox: the more we uncover, the more we realize the vastness of what remains shrouded in mystery. It is an ever-expanding frontier, where each answer begets a multitude of new questions, perpetuating an infinite cycle of exploration and discovery.

In this book, we embark on a captivating journey through the unsolvable problems that have perplexed and challenged the greatest minds throughout history. We will explore the boundaries of human knowledge and confront the inherent limitations that govern our understanding of the universe and ourselves.

From the enigmatic realm of quantum mechanics, where the very fabric of reality defies our intuition, to the intricacies of artificial intelligence and the quest for replicating human consciousness, we will navigate the uncharted territories that lie beyond the reach of our current comprehension.

We will delve into the profound philosophical quandaries that have puzzled thinkers for centuries, such as the nature of consciousness, the existence of free will, and the fundamental question of why there is something rather than nothing.

Through the lens of unsolvable problems in mathematics and computer science, we will unravel the intricate complexities that arise from the interplay of logic, computation, and the limitations of algorithmic reasoning.

Moreover, we will explore the unsolvable puzzles that permeate our everyday lives, from the paradoxes of decision-making and the intricacies of language to the mysteries of human cognition and the boundaries of our sensory perception.

As we journey through these realms of the unknown, we will encounter the pioneering minds that have shaped our understanding of the unsolvable, from the visionary work of Alan Turing and Kurt Gödel to the cutting-edge research of contemporary scientists and philosophers.

This book is not merely a catalogue of unsolved mysteries; it is a celebration of the human spirit's relentless pursuit of knowledge and a testament to the enduring allure of the unknown. Through these pages, we will confront the very boundaries of our understanding and embrace the humbling realization that the universe is infinitely more complex and profound than we can ever fully comprehend.

Yet, in this humility lies a profound wisdom – the recognition that the true essence of human inquiry lies not in the answers we find, but in the questions we ask and the journey we undertake. It is a journey that has no end, for the unsolvable problems that await us are as numerous as the stars in the night sky, each one a tantalizing beacon beckoning us to explore the uncharted depths of existence.

So, join us on this extraordinary odyssey, where we will confront the unsolvable, embrace the unknown, and revel in the boundless wonder of the cosmos. For it is in the pursuit of the unsolvable that we truly discover the infinite potential of the human mind and the enduring resilience of our insatiable thirst for knowledge.

TABLE OF CONTENTS

Chapter 1: The Unsolvable Problems 1

Chapter 2: The Pioneers of Computation 10

Chapter 3: Navigating the Spectrum from P to NP 17

Chapter 4: Chaos Theory and Complexity 25

Chapter 5: The Limits of Unsolvable Problems 36

Chapter 6: The Social and Theoretical Implications of Unsolvable Problems .. 41

Chapter 7: Gödel's Incompleteness Theorems 46

Chapter 8: The Domino Problem 50

Chapter 9: The Word Problem 54

Chapter 10: The Halting Problem 58

Chapter 11: The Post Correspondence Problem 63

Chapter 12: Bridging the Gap Between Logic and Reality 68

Chapter 13: Unsolvable Problems in Everyday Life 73

Chapter 14: The Prisoner's Dilemma 78

Chapter 15: The Paradox of Choice 82

Chapter 16: The Sorites Paradox 87

Chapter 17: The Post Correspondence Problem 91

Chapter 18: The Spectrum Problem 97

- Chapter 19: Richard's Paradox 103
- Chapter 20: The Kolmogorov Complexity 109
- Chapter 21: The Busy Beaver Problem 116
- Chapter 22: The Limits of Knowledge and Perception 122
- Chapter 23: The Boundaries of Knowledge 127
- Chapter 24: Language and Mathmatics 130
- Chapter 25: Asimov's Vision and the Ultimate Question 135
- Chapter 26: Mind, Information, and Omniscience 138
- Chapter 27: Incomprehensibility of Knowledge 142
- Chapter 28: The Constraints on Knowledge 146
- Chapter 29: The Infinite Possibilities of Knowledge 149
- Chapter 30: Evolution of Knowledge Expansion 152
- Chapter 31: Limits of Human Understanding 155
- Chapter 32: Types, Truths, and Theoretical Limits 158
- Chapter 33: Controversies of Inborn Understanding 161
- Chapter 34: Entscheidungsproblem 165
- Chapter 35: Millers Magical Number 168
- Chapter 36: The Ship of Theseus 171
- Chapter 37: Challenges of Achieving AGI 175
- Chapter 38: The Boundaries of Human Cognition 178
- Chapter 39: Neurological Cognitive Limitations 183
- Chapter 40: Limitations of Working Memory 187
- Chapter 41: Neural Mechanisms Underlying Limitations 191
- Chapter 42: Sensory Encoding and Hemifield Independence 196
- Chapter 43: Experimental Design and Analysis Methods 200

CHAPTER 1
THE UNSOLVABLE PROBLEMS

Imagine yourself deeply engrossed in the intricate labyrinth of a mathematical conundrum, your mind focused intently as you strive to unearth its elusive solution. Time ticks away, hours turning into days, weeks, even months. Yet, despite your unwavering determination and tenacity, you begin to grapple with an unsettling truth: the problem before you may be fundamentally unsolvable. This is the captivating and vexing territory of the unsolvable problem, a concept that has piqued the curiosity and perplexed the minds of computer scientists, mathematicians, and philosophers for generations.

The unsolvable problem is a paradox wrapped in an enigma, a tantalizing challenge that invites us to explore the very limits of our intellect and the capabilities of our computational systems. At the heart of this enigma lies the question: what makes some problems in computation uniquely unsolvable? In the pages that follow, we embark on an educational and thought-provoking journey through the world of unsolvable problems. We will delve into the historical backdrop of unsolvable problems, the theories and principles that underpin them, and their real-world implications. From the groundbreaking work of visionaries like Alan Turing and Kurt Gödel to the cutting-edge research of modern-day computer scientists, we will examine the fascinating evolution of our understanding of the unsolvable.

Our exploration will begin with the historical roots of computation, tracing back to pioneering figures like Alan Turing and Ada Lovelace. We will then introduce the central themes of unsolvable problems, such as Turing Completeness, the Halting Problem, P vs NP, and chaos theory. These topics will provide the foundation for understanding why some problems in computation remain unsolvable, and how they influence our daily lives, from software development to cryptography and beyond. Along the way, we will encounter mind-bending concepts like undecidability, computational complexity, and the limits of algorithmic problem-solving, all of which contribute to the rich tapestry of unsolvable problems.

Stay tuned as we unravel the mysteries of the unsolvable problem, shedding light on the historical, theoretical, and practical aspects of these fascinating conundrums. As you delve deeper into this complex and intriguing subject, you'll come to appreciate the profound implications of unsolvable problems and the ongoing quest to understand the very nature of knowledge itself. From the philosophical implications of Gödel's Incompleteness Theorems to the practical challenges of tackling NP-hard problems in fields like optimization and machine learning, the study of unsolvable problems promises to be an intellectually stimulating and deeply rewarding endeavor. So join us on this captivating journey as we explore the frontiers of the unsolvable and the enduring allure of the unknown.

In the captivating realm of computation, unsolvable problems assume a distinct importance, serving as the demarcation line between the attainable and the unreachable, the calculable and the enigmatic. These problems represent the limitations of what we can achieve with computers and, in turn, challenge our comprehension of computation and the very essence of problem-solving.

Unsolvable problems have been the subject of much intrigue and fascination since the inception of modern computation. Some of the most well-known unsolvable problems include the legendary Halting Problem posed by Alan Turing and the intricate conundrums that lie at the heart of chaos theory. As we delve deeper into these unsolvable problems, we will uncover both their historical, theoretical, and practical implications.

Delving deeper into the realm of unsolvable problems is an intellectually stimulating endeavor that promises to challenge our preconceptions about computation and problem-solving. From philosophical questions about the nature of reasoning and knowledge to practical concerns arising in fields like software engineering, artificial intelligence, and machine learning, unsolvable problems touch upon some of the most fundamental and socially relevant ideas of our time.

These intricate conundrums represent far more than mere abstract theoretical puzzles confined to the realm of mathematics. As we delve deeper into their implications and explore the depths of their complexities in depth, we will gain profound insights into the true capabilities and limitations of algorithms, computers, and even our own cognitive faculties.

We will confront the sobering possibility of problems that cannot be solved by any known computational means, whether classical or quantum, and ponder the implications of intractable complexity for everything from cryptography to forecasting chaotic systems.

In this journey through the captivating world of unsolvable problems, we will encounter many brilliant historical figures who helped shape modern computation as we know it today, from the inimitable Alan Turing and

THE UNSOLVABLE PROBLEM

Ada Lovelace to the pioneers of chaos theory. We will discover how breakthroughs in theory can lead to unexpected applications, just as obstacles encountered in practice often spur new theoretical insights in a virtuous cycle of progress.

Above all, we will develop a deeper appreciation for the intellectual allure and great societal significance of problems that remain unsolvable. While we may never find definitive or satisfying solutions to them, uncovering their true nature through arduous research promises to be an endlessly fascinating quest which will likely occupy scientists and thinkers for generations to come.

So, what precisely distinguishes an unsolvable problem from a solvable one? Is it merely a temporary deficiency in our current scientific understanding or a void in our collective knowledge that could someday be filled? Alternatively, could there be something inherent within the very nature of certain problems that makes them fundamentally impervious to solutions by any computational or logical means? These thought-provoking questions form the foundation of our exploration into the enigma of unsolvable problems. They invite us to ponder the limits of human intellect, the boundaries of what can be known, and the inherent complexities woven into the fabric of reality itself.

We will begin by tracing the historical backdrop of computation, starting with pioneering visionaries like Alan Turing, Ada Lovelace and others, and introduce the fundamental theories of computation that laid the groundwork for the universal Turing machine, a concept foundational to understanding what makes some problems unsolvable. Through their groundbreaking work, these luminaries paved the way for the digital revolution that has transformed every facet of modern life.

Following this, we will delve into the Halting Problem proposed by Turing himself, discussing its implications for software development and security.

We will explore how this seemingly abstract concept has profound consequences for the reliability and safety of the computer programs we rely on every day. Next, we will explore the intricacies of the P vs NP problem and its ramifications in cryptography, algorithm design, and daily technological applications. This problem, which questions the fundamental relationship between the difficulty of solving a problem and the difficulty of verifying a solution, has far-reaching implications for fields as diverse as cybersecurity, logistics, and artificial intelligence.

Venturing further into the realm of chaos theory, we will concentrate on its foundational principle: the sensitivity to initial conditions. We'll illustrate the profound influence of this principle on computational systems and modeling across diverse domains, including the predictive intricacies of meteorology and the fluctuating complexities of economic systems. Through fascinating examples and thought experiments, we will demonstrate how the slightest variations in input can lead to drastically divergent outcomes, underscoring the inherent unpredictability and complexity of many real-world systems.

Next, we will present a detailed examination of real-world applications and the challenges posed by unsolvable problems. Through a series of case studies, we'll delve into the realms of artificial intelligence and big data, considering the ethical quandaries that arise within the field of computing. Moreover, we will discuss the innovative strategies and practical workarounds that industry professionals have developed to mitigate the pervasive impact of unsolvable problems in various real-world contexts. From heuristic algorithms that provide approximate solutions to intractable problems, to the use of randomization and probabilistic techniques, we will explore the creative ways in which researchers and practitioners navigate the limitations imposed by unsolvable problems.

Moving on, we will discuss the social and ethical implications of unsolvable problems, including the limits of AI and the potential misuse of complexity for deception. We will also delve into the societal ramifications of problems that remain unsolvable, exploring how these limitations shape public policy, influence technological development, and challenge our understanding of what it means to live in an increasingly complex and interconnected world.

As we venture further into the intriguing realm of quantum computing and its potential to solve some of the unsolvable problems in classical computing, Chapter 7 of our scholarly work will delve into the principles and concepts of this complex field. Through accessible explanations, readers will gain a deeper understanding of quantum computing, piquing their intellectual curiosity. We will explore how the strange and counterintuitive properties of quantum systems, such as superposition and entanglement, may offer new avenues for tackling problems that have long confounded classical computers.

Moreover, this chapter will serve as an opportunity for introspection. We will engage in thought-provoking discussions centered around the philosophical implications of unsolvable problems, the nature of computation, and the limits of human knowledge. These profound discussions will add a new dimension to our understanding of the field and broaden the scope of this educational journey. We will contemplate the deeper questions that arise from grappling with the mysteries of unsolvable problems, considering how they challenge our fundamental assumptions about the nature of information, problem-solving, and the very boundaries of what can be known. Through these reflections, we will gain a richer appreciation for the beauty and complexity of the world around us, and the enduring human drive to push the frontiers of knowledge ever forward. By delving into the philosophical underpinnings of these unsolvable problems, we will uncover new insights into the nature of reality and the role of computation in shaping our understanding of it.

To facilitate a smoother reading experience, especially for those less familiar with the intricate terminology and concepts, we will also include a detailed glossary within the book. This invaluable resource will enable all readers to grasp the subject matter thoroughly and join us in our intellectual adventure. The glossary will serve as a handy reference guide, providing clear and concise definitions for the technical terms and concepts introduced throughout the book. By including this glossary, we ensure that readers from all backgrounds can engage with the material and fully participate in the fascinating exploration of quantum computing and its implications for solving unsolvable problems.

Prepare to embark on a captivating voyage through the intriguing landscape of unsolvable problems in computation. By exploring these profound enigmas together, we will uncover the deep-rooted mysteries that have long perplexed the greatest minds in science and philosophy. Our journey will take us through the annals of history, tracing the evolution of computational thought and the groundbreaking discoveries that have shaped our understanding of what is possible and what remains tantalizingly out of reach. Along the way, we will encounter the visionary thinkers and pioneers who have pushed the boundaries of computational theory, laying the foundation for the quantum revolution that promises to redefine the limits of what we can achieve.

Our expedition begins with an investigation of the historical background of computation, delving into the intellectual milieu that birthed the first computers and the foundational theories that underpin their functionality. Along the way, we will encounter pioneering figures like Alan Turing and Ada Lovelace, whose groundbreaking work set the stage for the computational revolution. We will explore the social, cultural, and technological contexts that shaped their ideas and the enduring impact of their contributions on the field of computer science. By understanding the historical roots of computation, we will gain a deeper appreciation for the remarkable progress that has been made and the challenges that remain.

As we progress, we will delve deeper into the most renowned unsolvable problems in computer science, starting with the Halting Problem, which Alan Turing first postulated. We will ponder the profound implications of this problem for software development and cybersecurity, as well as its significance in shaping the trajectory of computer science research. By examining the Halting Problem in detail, we will gain a deeper understanding of the fundamental limitations of computation and the ingenious ways in which researchers have sought to circumvent them. We will also consider the practical consequences of the Halting Problem for the development of reliable and secure software systems, highlighting the ongoing challenges and opportunities for innovation in this area.

Subsequently, we will explore the P versus NP problem, another major unsolvable problem in the realm of computation. We will endeavor to elucidate this enigmatic problem in an accessible manner, demonstrating its relevance to fields such as cryptography, algorithm design, and everyday technological applications. By demystifying the P versus NP problem, we will shed light on the profound implications it holds for the future of computing and the potential for quantum computing to provide new avenues for tackling this long-standing challenge. We will also consider the wider societal implications of the P versus NP problem, from the security of online transactions to the development of more efficient algorithms for solving complex problems in fields ranging from logistics to drug discovery.

In upcoming chapters, we will delve into the complexities of chaos theory, encounter real-world unsolvable problems, and contemplate the social and ethical implications of these unsolvable puzzles. Throughout our exploration, we will provide a "Further Reading" section at the end of each chapter, offering recommendations for books, articles, or online resources that offer a more in-depth understanding of the topics addressed. Additionally, a back-of-the-book glossary will be included to help non-expert readers navigate the technical terms and concepts presented, ensuring that the book remains accessible and engaging for a wide audience. By providing these additional resources and tools, we aim to create a comprehensive and immersive learning experience that will inspire readers to continue their exploration of the fascinating world of unsolvable problems in computation.

We'll venture beyond the computational realm, exploring unsolvable problems' manifestations across diverse fields like economics, meteorology, and cutting-edge AI systems. Our journey unveils the innovative strategies and clever workarounds professionals employ to navigate the challenges posed by unsolvable problems in real-world contexts, illuminating these abstract concepts' practical implications.

The primary goal is ensuring these complex ideas remain accessible to a general audience, regardless of prior computer science or mathematics knowledge. Readers from all backgrounds are invited on this thought-provoking odyssey, requiring only a curious mind and willingness to engage with the fascinating and challenging ideas arising at the intersection of computation, complexity, and chaos.

Explore the enigmatic intersection of computation, complexity, and chaos where unsolvable problems challenge assumptions and expand perspectives on our knowledge's limits.

CHAPTER 2
THE PIONEERS OF COMPUTATION

The story of computation is a testament to human ingenuity, a saga of the relentless pursuit to harness the power of information and push the boundaries of what is calculable. It begins in the early 19th century with the visionary English mathematician and inventor, Charles Babbage, who conceived of machines that would revolutionize the very concept of computation. Babbage's designs for the Difference Engine and later the Analytical Engine laid the conceptual framework for what would become the modern computer, envisioning a machine capable of executing any calculation that could be reduced to a series of logical operations, a device that could be programmed to carry out intricate sequences of instructions without human intervention. Though Babbage's ambitious projects were never fully realized in his lifetime, his groundbreaking ideas planted the seeds of the computational revolution that would blossom a century later.

Alongside Babbage stood Ada Lovelace, a brilliant mathematician and the daughter of the renowned poet Lord Byron. Lovelace possessed a rare combination of mathematical acumen and imaginative insight, enabling her to grasp the true potential of Babbage's machines. She recognized that these devices could be harnessed for far more than mere calculation - they could manipulate symbols, process logic, and even compose music. In essence, Lovelace foresaw the birth of programming, the art of instructing machines to carry out complex tasks. Her visionary writings on the Analytical Engine, including what is considered to be the first published algorithm, earned her the title of the world's first computer programmer. Lovelace's contributions underscored the boundless possibilities that computation held, hinting at a future where machines would become powerful tools for human expression and creativity.

As the 19th century gave way to the 20th, the torch of computational progress was passed to a new generation of pioneers. At the forefront of this new era stood Alan Turing, a brilliant British mathematician who would forever alter the landscape of computer science. Turing's groundbreaking work revolutionized the field, laying the foundation for the concept of universal computation - the revolutionary idea that a single machine, given the right instructions, could be programmed to solve any computable problem. This transformative theory became the bedrock upon which the edifice of modern computing was built, ushering in the digital age and reshaping the world as we know it.

Turing's landmark paper, "On Computable Numbers," published in 1936, introduced the concept of the Turing machine - a hypothetical device capable of performing any computation that could be done by a human following a set of predefined rules. The Turing machine consisted of an infinite tape divided into cells, a read-write head that could move along the tape, and a set of instructions that governed the machine's behavior based on the symbols it encountered. Despite its simplicity, the Turing machine proved to be a remarkably powerful model of computation, capable of simulating any algorithm that could be executed by a computer. Turing's work demonstrated that there were fundamental limits to what could be computed, but within those limits, a single universal machine could tackle any solvable problem.

Concurrently, on the other side of the Atlantic, the brilliant mathematician Alonzo Church was independently developing a parallel theory of computation, grounded in the elegant and powerful formalism of lambda calculus. Church's lambda calculus provided a theoretical framework for expressing and manipulating functions, serving as a foundation for the study of computability and laying the groundwork for the development of functional programming languages. The intellectual paths of Church and Turing converged, their pioneering research dovetailing in a remarkable confluence of ideas that gave rise to the landmark Church-Turing thesis.

The Church-Turing thesis stands as a profound and far-reaching conjecture in the annals of computer science, with implications that reverberate to this day. At its core, the thesis suggests that any effectively calculable function can be computed by a Turing machine or expressed in the lambda calculus. In other words, it proposes that the concepts of Turing computability and lambda-definability are equivalent, capturing the essence of what it means to be computable. The Church-Turing thesis has stood the test of time, withstanding rigorous scrutiny and serving as a guiding principle in the development of computational theory.

However, the Church-Turing thesis also hints at the existence of inherent limits to what can be computed, suggesting the presence of fundamental constraints that govern the universe of information processing. This revelation has profound consequences, challenging our assumptions about the capabilities and limitations of technology, and pushing us to grapple with the very nature of computation itself. It raises philosophical questions about the boundaries of human knowledge and the extent to which we can harness the power of machines to unravel the mysteries of the universe.

As we venture into the subsequent chapters, the groundbreaking work of pioneers such as Babbage, Lovelace, Turing, and Church will be revealed as the foundation for the computational revolution that restructured the 20th century. Their visionary insights and relentless pursuit of understanding laid the groundwork for the modern digital age, transforming the way we live, work, and interact with the world around us. However, their discoveries also hinted at the existence of a category of problems that would elude even the most sophisticated computational tools.

These are the unsolvable problems, the ciphers that encapsulate the essence of computation and the boundaries of human understanding. They represent the frontiers of knowledge, where the limits of our ability to process information become starkly apparent, and where the very foundations of our technological progress are called into question. From the halting problem to the intractability of certain computational tasks, these unsolvable problems serve as a humbling reminder of the complexity and depth of the computational universe.

The nature of these unsolvable problems will be explored in depth, delving into their origins, implications, and the profound questions they raise about the nature of computation and the limits of human knowledge. The philosophical and practical consequences of these computational conundrums will be grappled with, seeking to understand their impact on fields ranging from mathematics and computer science to physics and metaphysics.

Through this exploration, the beauty and intricacy of the computational landscape will be appreciated, marveling at the ingenuity of the pioneers who laid the foundation for the digital age, and confronting the fundamental limits that define the boundaries of what is computable. Navigating this complex terrain will lead to a deeper understanding of the nature of computation, the limits of human knowledge, and the enduring mysteries that continue to captivate and inspire in the pursuit of understanding. The very foundations of logic and mathematics are tested by these unsolvable problems, challenging long-held assumptions and forcing a reevaluation of what it means to compute, to understand, and to know.

As the journey through the history and implications of unsolvable problems unfolds, it becomes clear that these enigmas are not just abstract curiosities confined to the ivory towers of academia. They have far-reaching consequences that permeate every aspect of our increasingly digital world. From the security of our online transactions to the efficiency of our algorithms, from the development of artificial intelligence to the modeling of complex systems, unsolvable problems cast their shadow over the landscape of computation.

In cryptography, for example, the very notion of security often hinges on the intractability of certain mathematical problems. The difficulty of factoring large numbers or solving discrete logarithms forms the basis for widely used encryption schemes that protect our sensitive data. Yet, the specter of quantum computing looms on the horizon, threatening to upend these assumptions and render our current security measures obsolete. The race to develop post-quantum cryptography is a direct response to the unsolvable problems that underpin our digital security.

In the realm of optimization and decision-making, unsolvable problems manifest as the curse of dimensionality, the combinatorial explosion that renders many real-world problems computationally intractable. From scheduling and logistics to drug discovery and materials science, the sheer number of possible solutions grows exponentially with the size of the problem, quickly outpacing the capabilities of even the most powerful supercomputers. Heuristics and approximations become the tools of the trade, trading off optimality for feasibility in the face of unsolvable complexity.

As artificial intelligence and machine learning continue to advance at a breakneck pace, unsolvable problems take on new significance. The dream of creating truly intelligent machines, capable of reasoning, learning, and adapting like humans, is tempered by the realization that certain cognitive tasks may be fundamentally unsuited to computational approaches. The hard problem of consciousness, the question of whether machines can ever truly understand or experience the world as we do, remains an unsolved and perhaps unsolvable mystery at the intersection of computation, philosophy, and neuroscience.

In the study of complex systems, from the weather patterns that shape our climate to the economic forces that drive our markets, unsolvable problems rear their heads in the form of chaos and emergence. The sensitivity to initial conditions that characterizes chaotic systems renders long-term predictions effectively impossible, no matter how much computational power is brought to bear. The emergent properties that arise from the interactions of simple components, whether in the flocking of birds or the behavior of financial markets, defy reductionist analysis and challenge our ability to model and control the world around us.

As we grapple with these unsolvable problems and their implications, it becomes clear that they are not just limitations to be overcome, but also opportunities for discovery and innovation. By pushing against the boundaries of what is computable, by exploring the frontiers of complexity and emergence, we expand the horizons of human knowledge and open up new avenues for scientific and technological progress. In the face of unsolvable problems, we are forced to think creatively, to develop new paradigms and perspectives, and to embrace the inherent uncertainty and unpredictability of the world we inhabit.

Unsolvable problems are a reflection of the human condition, as we constantly strive to comprehend and control the world around us. This struggle highlights the incredible ability of the human mind to imagine the impossible and push the boundaries of what we know and accomplish. As we confront these complex challenges, we are reminded of the allure and enigma of the cosmos, and the indomitable human spirit that propels us relentlessly in the quest for knowledge and comprehension.

In the end, the significance of unsolvable problems lies not just in their technical details or their practical implications, but in the way they shape our understanding of ourselves and our place in the world. They remind us of the limits of our knowledge, the depths of our ignorance, and the vast uncharted territories that lie beyond the reach of our computational tools. Yet, they also inspire us to keep pushing forward, to keep asking questions, and to keep seeking new ways to make sense of the complex and chaotic world we inhabit.

CHAPTER 3

NAVIGATING THE SPECTRUM FROM P TO NP

As we delved into the Halting Problem in the preceding chapter, we glimpsed the existence of unsolvable computational enigmas that have puzzled researchers and computer scientists for decades. These problems, which defy a conclusive solution, highlight the fundamental limitations of classical computing and the inherent complexity of certain computational tasks. However, within the realm of solvable problems, a spectrum of complexity emerges. Some problems yield to swift solutions, even with extensive inputs, while others elude efficient resolution, requiring exponentially more time and resources to solve.

The P versus NP problem represents a fundamental challenge in computer science, seeking to uncover the intrinsic difference between problems that can be efficiently verified and those that can be efficiently solved. This long-standing conundrum has captivated researchers for decades, as its resolution would not only deepen our theoretical understanding of computation but also have far-reaching practical implications across various domains. From cryptography and optimization to decision-making and beyond, the P versus NP problem holds the key to unlocking new possibilities and pushing the boundaries of what we can achieve with computational power.

To truly appreciate the significance of the P versus NP problem, it is crucial to understand the concepts of "fast" and "efficient" in the context of computation. In the realm of computer science, the efficiency of an algorithm is not measured by its absolute running time but rather by how its running time grows in relation to the size of the input. An algorithm is considered "efficient" if its running time increases at a manageable rate as the input size grows larger. This property is often referred to as having a polynomial-time complexity, which means that the algorithm's running time can be expressed as a polynomial function of the input size. In other words, even as the input grows, the running time of an efficient algorithm will not explode exponentially but instead grow at a more controlled pace.

The distinction between polynomial-time complexity and exponential-time complexity is at the heart of the P versus NP problem. Problems that can be solved by algorithms with polynomial-time complexity are classified as belonging to the class P, which stands for "polynomial time." These problems are considered tractable and can be efficiently solved, even for large input sizes. On the other hand, problems for which no polynomial-time algorithm is known are classified as belonging to the class NP, which stands for "nondeterministic polynomial time." These problems may be efficiently verified but not necessarily efficiently solved.

In contrast, an "inefficient" algorithm would have an exponential-time complexity, where the running time grows exponentially with the input size. Such algorithms quickly become impractical for large inputs, as their runtimes can balloon to unmanageable levels, making them effectively unusable in many real-world applications. The increasing complexity can quickly render these algorithms infeasible, even for moderate input sizes.

The P versus NP problem seeks to determine whether problems with "quickly verifiable" solutions can also be "quickly solvable" by efficient, polynomial-time algorithms. This fundamental distinction lies at the heart of understanding the inherent limits of computational power and the potential for groundbreaking advancements in fields like cryptography, optimization, and decision-making. Resolving this long-standing question could have far-reaching implications for the development of more powerful and efficient algorithms.

The class P, denoting "polynomial time," encompasses problems addressable by efficient algorithms—ones with runtimes scaling polynomially with input size. These efficient algorithms are often favored for their predictable and manageable performance characteristics, making them reliable and practical choices for a wide range of applications. Familiar problems like sorting lists of numbers or determining the shortest path in a map fall within the realm of P, as they can be solved using well-understood polynomial-time techniques that ensure reasonable computation times, even for large-scale inputs.

Conversely, the class NP, standing for "nondeterministic polynomial time," comprises problems where solutions can be efficiently verified, even if finding these solutions proves arduous. In other words, while the solutions to NP problems can be quickly checked, the process of actually discovering those solutions may require an impractically long time. An exemplar of an NP problem is the Traveling Salesman dilemma: given a roster of cities and their intercity distances, deduce the shortest path visiting each city exactly once. This problem is known to be computationally difficult, as the number of possible routes grows exponentially with the number of cities. The challenge lies in the fact that as the number of cities increases, the number of potential paths to explore explodes, making it infeasible to exhaustively check every possible route to find the optimal one. This exponential growth in complexity is a hallmark of many NP problems, setting them apart from the more tractable problems in P.

At the heart of the matter, the P versus NP conundrum is centered around a deceptively simple yet profound question: are these two classes, in fact, one and the same? To put it another way, does the capacity for efficient verification of solutions indicate that the problems themselves can be resolved with equal efficiency? If P were equal to NP, it would imply that every problem for which a solution can be quickly verified could also have that solution found quickly. This would have far-reaching consequences across various domains, from cryptography and cybersecurity to optimization and artificial intelligence. Many problems that are currently considered intractable would suddenly become solvable, revolutionizing entire fields of study and application.

This enigmatic question is a cornerstone of computational complexity theory, a field that delves into the intricate dance between the verification of solutions and the discovery of those solutions across a wide spectrum of mathematical problems. The theory probes the possibility of a world where every problem that allows for its solutions to be rapidly authenticated could also be swiftly and directly solved. Despite the question's seeming simplicity, it has eluded definitive proof for years, leaving countless theorists in its wake, grappling with its implications. The pursuit of an answer has led to the development of sophisticated mathematical techniques and the exploration of deep connections between seemingly disparate areas of mathematics and computer science. The P versus NP problem has become a lens through which researchers investigate the fundamental nature of computation and the limits of what can be efficiently computed. Its resolution, whether in the affirmative or negative, would mark a significant milestone in our understanding of the computational universe and its boundaries.

The question of whether P equals NP cuts to the core of our understanding of computational efficiency and the nature of problem-solving itself. It asks whether the ability to quickly verify the correctness of a solution to a problem necessarily implies the existence of an equally efficient method for finding that solution in the first place. This inquiry has profound implications for a wide range of fields, from cryptography and optimization to artificial intelligence and beyond. The answer, whether affirmative or negative, would fundamentally reshape our understanding of the limits of computation and the nature of algorithmic problem-solving.

Many computer scientists lean towards the negative, positing that NP harbors problems beyond the reach of P. They conjecture that the two complexity classes do not coincide, and that NP contains inherently harder problems that are fundamentally more challenging to solve efficiently. However, despite extensive endeavors spanning generations of researchers, no definitive proof has emerged to conclusively settle this longstanding question. This enduring query lingers, promising profound repercussions for the theory and practice of computation upon its final resolution.

The quest for a resolution to the P versus NP problem has driven the development of entire subfields of theoretical computer science, from the study of approximation algorithms and hardness of approximation to the exploration of interactive proof systems and probabilistically checkable proofs. These areas of research have not only shed light on the nature of computational complexity but have also yielded powerful tools and techniques with applications far beyond the scope of the P versus NP question itself. The problem has served as a catalyst for innovation and discovery, pushing the boundaries of our understanding of computation and its limits.

The implications of the P versus NP problem stretch far beyond the confines of computer science, extending into the realms of mathematics, cryptography, economics, and other disciplines where computational modeling and algorithm design play central roles. Both a positive and negative resolution of this question could reshape our fundamental understanding of the possibilities and limitations of efficient computation. For now, the P versus NP problem endures as one of the great open challenges at the intersection of mathematics and computer science, captivating the attention of scholars and practitioners alike.

A world in which P equals NP would be a radically different one from the computational landscape we currently inhabit. It would imply that every problem for which a solution can be efficiently verified could also be efficiently solved, erasing the distinction between the complexity classes that has long been a foundational assumption of computer science. This would have far-reaching consequences for fields such as cryptography, where the security of many widely used protocols relies on the presumed difficulty of certain NP-complete problems. In an era where digital security is of paramount importance, the resolution of the P versus NP problem could have significant practical implications for the way we protect our sensitive data and communications.

Should P be shown to equal NP, a paradigm shift would ensue, rendering problems currently deemed arduous in fields like optimization, artificial intelligence, and cryptography effortlessly solvable through the development of efficient algorithms. Conversely, if P is proven not to equal NP (as is widely believed), it would signal inherent limitations in efficient computation, delineating a profound dichotomy in the nature of computational challenges and their underlying complexity.

The ramifications of the P versus NP problem are not limited to the realm of theoretical computer science. In fields such as operations research and artificial intelligence, the ability to efficiently solve certain classes of optimization problems could revolutionize the way we approach tasks such as resource allocation, scheduling, and machine learning. The resolution of this question could also have significant implications for our understanding of the nature of human problem-solving and the potential for artificial systems to match or exceed human cognitive capabilities in certain domains.

The P versus NP debate is closely intertwined with the field of cryptography. Modern encryption systems, such as the widely used RSA protocol for online security, rely on the assumed complexity of certain NP problems. A convergence of P and NP would jeopardize the security of these cryptographic mechanisms, potentially rendering them vulnerable to efficient attacks.

Despite the immense theoretical and practical significance of the P versus NP problem, it remains one of the most elusive and challenging open problems in computer science. Generations of researchers have grappled with this question, developing increasingly sophisticated techniques and proof strategies in an attempt to settle the debate once and for all. Yet, despite these efforts, a definitive resolution continues to elude us, leaving the problem as an enduring mystery that continues to inspire and frustrate researchers in equal measure.

Despite its deep theoretical roots, the P versus NP problem reverberates with practical implications that extend far beyond the confines of academia. The Clay Mathematics Institute has spotlighted this question as one of mathematics' seven paramount open challenges, offering a million-dollar reward for its definitive resolution. The potential impact of this problem on fields ranging from optimization to national security has fueled ongoing research and debate among the world's leading scholars and practitioners.

As we continue to push the boundaries of computational complexity theory, the P versus NP problem remains a guiding light, illuminating the frontiers of our understanding and driving us to explore ever more deeply the nature of efficient computation. Whether a resolution lies just around the corner or remains a distant goal, the pursuit of an answer to this profound question will undoubtedly continue to shape the landscape of theoretical computer science for generations to come.

In the forthcoming chapter, we will navigate a domain where computational boundaries intersect with the intricate tapestry of real-world intricacies: the realm of chaos and complexity theory. This exploration will shed further light on the fundamental nature of computational challenges and the limits of efficient problem-solving, building upon the foundational concepts introduced in the discussion of the P versus NP problem.

As we embark on this journey into the heart of computational complexity, it is worth reflecting on the profound implications of the questions we seek to answer. The P versus NP problem is not merely an abstract theoretical construct, but a deeply fundamental inquiry into the nature of problem-solving itself. Its resolution, in whichever direction it may ultimately fall, promises to reshape our understanding of the very foundations of computation and the limits of what we can hope to achieve through algorithmic means.

Yet, even in the face of this daunting challenge, we press on, driven by the innate human desire to unravel the mysteries of the universe and to push the boundaries of our understanding ever further. The P versus NP problem may still lie beyond our grasp, but the pursuit of its resolution continues to illuminate the path forward, guiding us towards new insights, new discoveries, and a deeper appreciation of the fundamental nature of computation itself.

CHAPTER 4
CHAOS THEORY AND COMPLEXITY

The exploration of unsolvable problems and computational complexity has illuminated the boundaries of computation, revealing its inherent limitations in tackling certain challenges. However, another realm of inquiry presents a unique form of restriction: the examination of chaos and complexity.

Chaos theory, a fascinating branch of mathematics, delves into the analysis of systems that exhibit extreme sensitivity to the minutest of initial conditions. In such systems, even an infinitesimal alteration can trigger a cascade of events leading to outcomes that are staggeringly different from the original scenario. This unpredictable behavior arises from the intricate interplay of multiple variables within the system, each influencing and being influenced by the others in a continuous feedback loop.

A classic example of chaos in action is the weather. Minute variations in atmospheric pressure, temperature, or humidity can snowball into vastly

THE UNSOLVABLE PROBLEM

different weather patterns, making long-term weather prediction an inherently challenging task. The butterfly effect, a popular metaphor in chaos theory, aptly illustrates this concept. The notion suggests that a butterfly flapping its wings in one part of the world could, in theory, set off a chain reaction that culminates in a hurricane forming on the other side of the globe.

The implications of chaos theory for computation are profound. It highlights the inherent limitations of deterministic models in accurately predicting the behavior of complex systems. In such systems, even the most sophisticated models can be thrown off course by unforeseen, minuscule changes in initial conditions. This inherent unpredictability poses significant challenges for various computational tasks, including weather forecasting, economic modeling, and even the design of secure cryptographic systems.

Yet, chaos theory also presents opportunities. By understanding the underlying principles of chaotic systems, we can develop strategies to mitigate their unpredictable nature. One approach involves focusing on statistical predictions rather than attempting to pinpoint exact outcomes. Another strategy entails identifying key control parameters within the system that can be manipulated to influence its overall behavior.

The study of chaos and complexity adds another layer to our understanding of the limits of computation. It reminds us that not all problems can be solved with brute computational force and that embracing the inherent unpredictability of certain systems is crucial for navigating the complexities of our world.

The field of meteorology offers a compelling illustration of this principle. Predicting weather patterns hinges upon a complex and delicately balanced system of atmospheric conditions, where seemingly insignificant modifications can lead to dramatically different outcomes. A minor shift in temperature or pressure can, over time, translate into a significantly different weather pattern. This phenomenon is often captured through the metaphor of the "butterfly effect," which posits that the simple act of a butterfly fluttering its wings could set in motion a chain of events that ultimately influences the trajectory of a hurricane weeks later. This highlights the inherent sensitivity of chaotic systems to initial conditions, where seemingly trivial variations can have profound and far-reaching consequences.

In the intricate tapestry of computational systems, chaos theory weaves a fascinating thread, revealing a hidden world of unpredictable behavior. Seemingly insignificant modifications, like a subtle shift in input or a minor alteration in the algorithm, can trigger a cascade of dramatic changes, echoing the famed butterfly effect. This sensitivity to initial conditions, a hallmark of chaotic systems, manifests as a snowballing divergence in outcomes over time.

Consider the realm of weather prediction, where minute discrepancies in initial data can spiral into vastly different forecasts days or weeks later. This underscores the inherent unpredictability of complex systems and the challenges of replicating results in simulations. Robust algorithms, capable of handling such inherent variability, become crucial for navigating this intricate landscape.

The implications of chaos theory extend beyond weather prediction, influencing diverse fields such as cryptography, economics, and even the study of biological systems. It serves as a reminder of the inherent limitations of computational models and the importance of embracing complexity in our understanding of the world.

Many real-world systems, from the intricate workings of the human brain to the sprawling dynamics of global economics, exhibit the hallmarks of complex systems. These systems are characterized by a multitude of interacting components, where the emergent behavior of the whole cannot be readily predicted from the properties of its individual parts. Studying these systems often involves building computational models and simulations, seeking to unravel the underlying mechanisms and predict their future trajectories. However, the inherent complexity of these systems poses a significant challenge to computational approaches.

Even the most sophisticated computational models can struggle to capture the full richness and dynamism of complex systems. This is because the sheer number of interacting components and the intricate feedback loops within these systems can quickly overwhelm traditional computational methods. Moreover, the inherent stochasticity and non-linearity of complex systems often lead to emergent behaviors that are highly sensitive to initial conditions, a phenomenon known as chaos. This sensitivity implies that even minute variations in the initial state of the system can lead to vastly different outcomes, making long-term predictions highly challenging, if not impossible.

The study of complex systems has led to the development of novel computational techniques, such as agent-based modeling and artificial neural networks. These approaches attempt to overcome the limitations of traditional methods by simulating the behavior of individual agents or components within the system, rather than attempting to model the entire system as a monolithic entity. Agent-based models, for instance, represent the system as a collection of interacting agents, each with its own set of rules and behaviors, allowing for the emergence of complex global patterns from the interactions of these individual agents. Artificial neural networks, inspired by the structure and function of the human brain, are capable of learning and adapting to complex data patterns, making them suitable for modeling systems with high degrees of non-linearity and interdependence.

Despite these advances, the inherent complexity of many real-world systems places fundamental limits on what can be achieved with computation. Just as the Halting Problem demonstrates the existence of inherently unsolvable problems in computer science, the study of chaos and complexity suggests that some systems may be inherently unpredictable, regardless of the sophistication of our computational tools. This realization underscores the importance of adopting a humble approach to modeling complex systems, acknowledging the inherent limitations of computation and focusing on understanding the qualitative dynamics and emergent properties of these systems, rather than seeking precise quantitative predictions. By embracing this approach, we can gain valuable insights into the workings of complex systems, even in the face of inherent unpredictability.

The exploration of chaos and complexity theory has far-reaching implications beyond the realm of computation. It challenges our understanding of causality, predictability, and the nature of knowledge itself. The realization that even deterministic systems can exhibit inherently unpredictable behavior forces us to grapple with the limits of our ability to understand and control the world around us. It invites us to embrace a more holistic and adaptive approach to problem-solving, one that recognizes the inherent complexity and interconnectedness of the systems we seek to understand and influence.

In the context of unsolvable problems, chaos and complexity theory offer valuable insights into the nature of the challenges we face. They remind us that some problems may be inherently intractable, not due to a lack of computational power or clever algorithms, but because of the fundamental properties of the systems they involve. This understanding can help us approach these problems with a sense of humility and realism, focusing our efforts on managing and adapting to complexity rather than seeking to eliminate it entirely.

Moreover, the study of chaos and complexity highlights the importance of interdisciplinary collaboration in tackling unsolvable problems. The insights and tools developed in fields such as mathematics, physics, and biology can offer valuable perspectives on the challenges we face in computation and beyond. By fostering cross-disciplinary dialogue and collaboration, we can develop more robust and adaptive approaches to dealing with the inherent complexity of the world around us.

Ultimately, the exploration of chaos and complexity invites us to embrace a more nuanced and dynamic understanding of the world, one that recognizes the inherent limitations of our knowledge and the importance of adaptive, context-dependent problem-solving. By doing so, we can develop more resilient and effective strategies for navigating the challenges of an increasingly complex and interconnected world, even in the face of unsolvable problems.

The ethical implications of dealing with unsolvable problems cannot be overlooked. As we confront the limits of computation and the inherent unpredictability of complex systems, we must grapple with the potential consequences of our actions and decisions. In a world where some problems may be fundamentally intractable, how do we ensure that our efforts to manage and mitigate complexity are guided by a strong ethical framework?

One key consideration is the importance of transparency and accountability. When dealing with unsolvable problems, it is crucial that we are honest and upfront about the limitations of our knowledge and the potential risks and uncertainties involved. This means being transparent about the assumptions and limitations of our models and simulations, and acknowledging the inherent unpredictability of the systems we seek to understand and influence. It also means being accountable for the decisions we make based on these models and simulations, and being willing to adapt and revise our approaches in light of new evidence or changing circumstances.

Another important ethical consideration is the need to prioritize the well-being of those who are most vulnerable to the impacts of unsolvable problems. In many cases, the complexity and unpredictability of these problems can have disproportionate impacts on marginalized and underserved communities, who may lack the resources and resilience to adapt to rapidly changing circumstances. As we seek to manage and mitigate the effects of unsolvable problems, we must ensure that our efforts are guided by a commitment to social justice and equity, and that we prioritize the needs and perspectives of those who are most affected.

Finally, dealing with unsolvable problems requires a deep sense of humility and a willingness to embrace uncertainty. In a world where some challenges may be fundamentally intractable, we must be willing to acknowledge the limits of our knowledge and the inherent unpredictability of the systems we seek to understand. This means approaching problem-solving with a spirit of curiosity and openness, and being willing to adapt and revise our strategies in light of new insights and changing circumstances. It also means cultivating a sense of resilience and adaptability, recognizing that in a complex and unpredictable world, the ability to respond and adapt to change is often more valuable than the pursuit of perfect solutions.

Ultimately, the ethical implications of dealing with unsolvable problems are complex and multifaceted, requiring ongoing dialogue and reflection among researchers, policymakers, and the broader public. By embracing a commitment to transparency, accountability, social justice, and humility, we can develop more responsible and effective approaches to managing the inherent complexity and unpredictability of the world around us, even in the face of seemingly intractable challenges.

These theoretical concepts, while fascinating in their own right, take on a new level of significance when applied to real-world situations. In the upcoming chapter, we'll dive into specific case studies that demonstrate how computational complexity and unsolvable problems manifest in various domains, from computer science and mathematics to economics, biology, and beyond. By examining these practical examples, we'll gain a deeper understanding of the challenges and opportunities presented by the limits of computation.

One particularly compelling case study involves the field of cryptography, where the security of our digital communications and transactions relies on the inherent difficulty of certain mathematical problems. We'll explore how the concept of one-way functions, which are easy to compute but difficult to invert, forms the basis for many cryptographic systems. However, we'll also see how the potential development of quantum computers, with their ability to tackle certain problems exponentially faster than classical computers, could upend the security of these systems, forcing researchers to develop new, post-quantum cryptographic techniques.

Another area where unsolvable problems arise is in the realm of optimization, where the goal is to find the best solution among a vast array of possibilities. From routing delivery trucks to optimizing investment portfolios, many real-world problems involve finding the most efficient or cost-effective solution. However, as the number of variables and constraints grows, the complexity of these problems can quickly become intractable, leading to the development of various approximation algorithms and heuristics.

In the biological sciences, the study of complex systems such as ecosystems, neural networks, and gene regulatory networks often runs up against the limits of computational modeling. We'll explore how researchers are using techniques from chaos theory and complexity science to gain insights into these systems, even in the absence of precise, predictive models.

Throughout these case studies, we'll also highlight the strategies and workarounds developed by practitioners to mitigate the impact of unsolvable problems. From embracing probabilistic and approximation algorithms to leveraging the power of distributed computing and crowdsourcing, we'll see how innovative approaches can help us make progress even in the face of seemingly intractable challenges.

In the relentless pursuit of solutions to unsolvable problems, researchers and practitioners have devised several innovative strategies. These methods, which include probabilistic and approximation algorithms, distributed computing, and crowdsourcing, demonstrate that while some problems may defy complete resolution, significant progress can still be achieved. This chapter delves into these ingenious approaches, illustrating how they enable us to navigate the complexities of intractable challenges effectively.

Probabilistic algorithms are a cornerstone in the toolkit for tackling computational problems where deterministic methods falter. Unlike deterministic algorithms, which provide precise results, probabilistic algorithms make decisions based on chance, which can be particularly effective when dealing with complex, dynamic systems. These algorithms are crucial in fields such as cryptography, where randomness ensures security, and machine learning, where they help manage enormous datasets with inherent uncertainties.

Closely related are approximation algorithms, designed to find near-optimal solutions when exact answers are unfeasible. These algorithms are invaluable in addressing NP-hard problems, where exact solutions require non-polynomial time. For instance, in logistics and network design, approximation algorithms help solve large-scale routing problems that are critical for global supply chains, providing solutions that are "good enough" and computationally feasible.

Distributed computing represents another promising frontier in the enduring quest to overcome seemingly unsolvable problems in computation. By distributing computational tasks across multiple computers or nodes in a network, this innovative approach aims to harness the immense collective processing power of interconnected systems to tackle problems that are simply too large or complex for any single machine to handle alone. Impactful projects like SETI@home, which utilizes idle computing resources from volunteers' personal devices to analyze radio signals for signs of extraterrestrial intelligence, and Folding@home, which simulates protein folding on a massive scale to aid medical research, demonstrate the formidable potential of distributed computing to expand the boundaries of what is possible.

This distributed model not only provides vastly greater computational capabilities through parallelization, but also enables more efficient data processing and analysis. By spreading workloads across many nodes, distributed systems can achieve much quicker iterations and explore multitudes of hypotheses simultaneously and in tandem. This is particularly advantageous in data-intensive fields like climate modeling and particle physics, where complex experiments can generate astronomical datasets on the scale of petabytes. Distributed approaches empower researchers to work with immense volumes of data, identify meaningful patterns and insights, and accelerate the pace of discovery.

In a similar vein, crowdsourcing leverages the collective knowledge, skills, and creative insights of large groups of people, typically over the internet, to help solve multifaceted problems and gather diverse information at scale. This method has transformed problem-solving and innovation in several scientific domains by successfully integrating human intelligence into computational processes. For instance, in bioinformatics, crowdsourcing platforms allow non-experts to participate in complex protein-folding puzzles - like the game Foldit - where players have proven adept at solving molecular structures faster than even the most sophisticated algorithms.

Moreover, crowdsourcing has become instrumental in generating the human-annotated data necessary for training machine learning algorithms and developing AI systems. By outsourcing data labeling tasks to many contributors, researchers can rapidly build the large, high-quality training datasets that enable more capable AI. This not only enhances the performance of algorithms, but also democratizes participation in scientific research, opening up opportunities for people across the globe to meaningfully contribute to innovation and discovery.

Often, the most significant leaps forward arise when these collaborative methods are combined in creative ways. For example, distributed computing can be implemented to run probabilistic algorithms at immense scale, while crowdsourcing helps iteratively refine their parameters through human-in-the-loop feedback. This synergy amplifies the complementary strengths of each approach, unlocking their latent potential and paving the way for breakthroughs in solving multifaceted computational problems. As the scale and complexity of the challenges we face grow, so too must our willingness to explore unorthodox solutions by connecting machines and crowds.

By grounding our exploration of computational complexity and unsolvable problems in real-world examples, we'll gain a richer understanding of how these abstract concepts play out in practice.

CHAPTER 5
THE LIMITS OF UNSOLVABLE PROBLEMS

Throughout this book, we've explored some of the most profound and abstract ideas in the theory of computation - ideas like the Halting Problem, computational complexity, and the chaotic behavior of complex systems. But these ideas are not just intellectual curiosities. They have real, practical implications for the challenges we face in the world today.

One area where we see the impact of unsolvable problems is in the field of artificial intelligence. As AI systems become more advanced and are applied to more complex domains, we increasingly run into the limits of what can be computed. For instance, training a large language model on a massive dataset of text and code can lead to impressive results, such as generating creative content or writing different kinds of computer programs. However, these models can also exhibit unexpected biases or generate outputs that are factually incorrect. Understanding the limitations of these models and the potential risks they pose is crucial for developing safe and responsible AI systems.

Another area where we encounter unsolvable problems is in the realm of cryptography. Cryptographic systems are designed to protect sensitive information from unauthorized access, and they rely on complex mathematical problems that are believed to be computationally intractable. However, advances in computing power and the development of new algorithms could potentially threaten the security of these systems. It is therefore essential for cryptographers to stay ahead of these advancements and develop new cryptographic methods that can withstand future attacks.

Finally, the study of unsolvable problems has profound implications for our understanding of the world around us. Chaotic systems, for example, are ubiquitous in nature, from the weather to the stock market. These systems are highly sensitive to initial conditions, meaning that even small changes can lead to vastly different outcomes. This makes it extremely difficult to predict the long-term behavior of these systems, and it highlights the limitations of our ability to control and manipulate complex systems.

By understanding the nature of unsolvable problems, we gain a deeper appreciation for the challenges and opportunities that lie ahead in the fields of artificial intelligence, cryptography, and scientific modeling. It also reminds us of the fundamental limits of computation and the importance of humility in the face of complexity.

Consider the challenge of creating an AI system to diagnose diseases based on medical scans. On the surface, this might seem like a straightforward problem of pattern recognition. But medical diagnosis is an inherently complex and uncertain process, often requiring the integration of multiple pieces of evidence and the application of expert judgment. Creating an AI system that can fully replicate this process may run into fundamental limits of computability and complexity.

Similar challenges arise in fields like autonomous vehicles, where AI systems must navigate complex and unpredictable environments. Factors such as weather conditions, unexpected obstacles, and human behavior can introduce a level of uncertainty that is difficult for even the most sophisticated algorithms to account for.

In financial modeling, the complexity of economic systems can make precise predictions impossible. Economic models rely on assumptions about human behavior, global events, and market trends, all of which are inherently unpredictable. Even the slightest variations in these factors can lead to significant deviations from projected outcomes.

Another area where unsolvable problems arise is in cybersecurity. Many modern cryptographic systems rely on the presumed difficulty of certain computational problems. However, the emergence of quantum computing has cast doubt on the long-term viability of these systems. Quantum computers have the potential to solve certain problems that are intractable for classical computers, including those that underpin many modern encryption methods. This raises concerns about the security of sensitive data in the future.

Moreover, the inherent complexity of software systems means that it may be impossible to create perfectly secure software. Just as the Halting Problem shows that there are limits to what can be computed, the complexity of software suggests that there may always be unknown vulnerabilities and bugs. Despite rigorous testing and quality assurance measures, unexpected interactions between components or unforeseen circumstances can lead to security breaches. This stark reality highlights the ongoing challenge of securing software in a world of ever-evolving threats and underscores the need for constant vigilance and adaptation.

Navigating the realm of unsolvable problems requires a profound shift in perspective - accepting that certain problems may remain unsolvable, at least with our current understanding and computational capabilities. This shift in perspective allows us to focus on developing practical solutions that mitigate risks and optimize outcomes within the constraints of computational limitations. By embracing the inherent complexity of the world, we can navigate the challenges posed by unsolvable problems and continue to advance our understanding and utilization of computation in meaningful ways.

Ultimately, grappling with unsolvable problems in the real world demands a shift in mindset. Rather than seeing the limits of computation as an impenetrable barrier, we can view them as a guide, helping us to focus our efforts and set realistic expectations aligned with the realities of computational theory. We can also explore the potential of human-computer collaboration, where humans and machines work together symbiotically to solve problems that are intractable for either alone. By embracing the inherent complexity of computation and adopting a more nuanced understanding of its limitations, we can navigate the challenges posed by unsolvable problems and continue to advance our understanding of the world around us, pushing the boundaries of what is possible with a judicious combination of human ingenuity and computational power.

Furthermore, accepting the existence of these unsolvable problems fosters a more realistic perspective on the capabilities and limitations of technology. This can lead to more responsible development and deployment of computational tools, ensuring that they are used ethically and effectively within their boundaries.

By comprehending the inherent limitations of computational capabilities, we foster a more profound understanding of the intricate nature of our world and the challenges we encounter. By accepting and embracing this complexity, we unlock new avenues, paving the way for innovative solutions that challenge and redefine the boundaries of feasibility. Recognizing the existence of unsolvable problems does not imply defeat, but rather serves as an impetus for continued exploration and inquiry.

Accepting these limitations encourages us to think beyond traditional problem-solving methodologies, to seek alternative strategies, and to push the limits of what is achievable. It is through this nuanced understanding of computation's constraints that we can harness its true potential, collaborating with human ingenuity to address issues that would otherwise remain intractable. By acknowledging the existence of unsolvable problems, we are empowered to navigate the realm of computational complexity with greater clarity and purpose, ultimately expanding the frontiers of human knowledge and capabilities.

CHAPTER 6

THE SOCIAL AND THEORETICAL IMPLICATIONS OF UNSOLVABLE PROBLEMS

As we've explored throughout this book, unsolvable problems and computational complexity have far-reaching implications that extend beyond the realm of pure mathematics and computer science. These concepts shape our understanding of the fundamental limits of computation and, by extension, the boundaries of what we can achieve with technology. In this chapter, we'll examine the social and theoretical implications of unsolvable problems, delving into how they impact various domains and the challenges they present.

One area where unsolvable problems have significant ramifications is artificial intelligence. As AI systems become increasingly sophisticated and are applied to more complex tasks, we inevitably encounter the limitations imposed by computational complexity. For instance, many optimization problems that arise in AI, such as finding the optimal configuration of a neural network or determining the best strategy for a game, are known to be NP-hard. This means that as the size of the problem grows, the time required to find an optimal solution increases exponentially, quickly becoming intractable even for the most powerful computers.

The existence of such unsolvable problems in AI has important implications for the development and deployment of these systems. It suggests that there may be fundamental limits to what AI can achieve, regardless of advances in hardware or algorithms. It also highlights the need for AI researchers and practitioners to develop strategies for coping with intractability, such as using approximation algorithms or heuristics that can find good, albeit suboptimal, solutions in a reasonable amount of time.

Another domain where unsolvable problems loom large is cryptography. Modern cryptographic systems rely on the presumed difficulty of certain mathematical problems, such as integer factorization or the discrete logarithm problem. These problems are believed to be "hard" in the sense that no efficient algorithm is known to solve them for large instances. This hardness is what underlies the security of popular encryption schemes like RSA and Diffie-Hellman.

However, the security of these cryptographic systems is continually under threat as new algorithms and computing paradigms emerge. The development of quantum computers, in particular, has the potential to upend the field of cryptography. Quantum algorithms like Shor's algorithm can, in theory, efficiently solve problems like integer factorization, rendering many current encryption methods obsolete. This has spurred a surge of interest in post-quantum cryptography, which seeks to develop cryptographic primitives that are secure against both classical and quantum computers.

The specter of unsolvable problems also looms large in the field of software verification. As software systems become increasingly complex, with millions of lines of code and countless interactions between components, ensuring their correctness and reliability becomes a daunting challenge. Formal verification methods, which use mathematical techniques to prove that a program satisfies certain properties, offer a rigorous approach to this problem. However, the undecidability of the halting problem and Rice's theorem, which states that any non-trivial property of the behavior of a Turing machine is undecidable, pose fundamental limits to what can be automatically verified.

This has led to the development of various approaches to circumvent these limitations, such as using interactive theorem provers that rely on human guidance, or focusing on specific, decidable fragments of program behavior. Yet, the core challenge remains: ensuring the correctness and security of complex software systems in the face of unsolvable problems is an ongoing struggle that requires a combination of theoretical advances, practical tools, and human ingenuity.

Beyond these specific domains, the study of unsolvable problems and computational complexity has broader implications for our understanding of the nature of computation and the limits of human knowledge. It reveals that there are fundamental boundaries to what we can achieve with computation, no matter how powerful our machines become. It also highlights the importance of embracing heuristics, approximations, and probabilistic methods in tackling complex computational problems, as waiting for an optimal solution may be infeasible or even impossible.

Moreover, the existence of unsolvable problems serves as a humbling reminder of the vastness and complexity of the mathematical universe. It suggests that there are truths that lie beyond the reach of any computational system, and that human intuition and creativity will always play a crucial role in pushing the boundaries of what we can know and understand.

As we delve deeper into the realm of unsolvable problems, it becomes evident that these challenges are not merely hurdles to be overcome but also gateways to a more profound understanding of computation and knowledge itself. This chapter expands on the implications of these problems for the very nature of human inquiry and the computational limits imposed on us, exploring further the truths that lie beyond our current capabilities and the strategies we might employ to approach them.

The mathematical universe is vast and filled with complexities that stretch beyond the current understanding of computational and algorithmic methods. This vastness suggests that there are entire realms of mathematical truth that remain unexplored and that these truths may hold the key to solving some of the most pressing problems in science and philosophy. The exploration of these areas often requires a combination of computational experimentation, theoretical insight, and creative conjecture.

Given the limitations of both human and computational problem-solving, a collaborative approach that synergizes both can lead to better outcomes. Hybrid systems that integrate human intuition with algorithmic efficiency can tackle complex problems more effectively than either approach alone. For instance, in the domain of complex decision-making, combining machine learning algorithms with human oversight can optimize outcomes while mitigating risks associated with automated systems.

Finally, the discussion of unsolvable problems invites us to consider their broader philosophical implications. These problems challenge our understanding of the scope and limits of human knowledge and prompt us to question the epistemological foundations of science and technology. They remind us that while our computational tools are powerful, they are ultimately tools—extensions of the human intellect, not replacements for it.

This chapter not only broadens our comprehension of the computational challenges we face but also inspires a deeper appreciation for the intellectual and creative pursuits that define the human condition. It is in this spirit that we continue to explore, discover, and ultimately transcend the boundaries of the known.

CHAPTER 7
GÖDEL'S INCOMPLETENESS THEOREMS

In our exploration of the limits of computation, we have thus far focused primarily on the work of pioneers like Alan Turing and Alonzo Church, whose ideas laid the foundation for the modern theory of computation. However, there is another figure whose contributions are equally profound and far-reaching, not just for computer science, but for the very foundations of mathematics and logic itself. That figure is Kurt Gödel, and his incompleteness theorems represent a landmark in 20th-century thought that continues to shape our understanding of the nature of truth and provability.

Gödel, an Austrian-American mathematician and logician, published his incompleteness theorems in 1931, at the young age of 25. These theorems, which he proved using ingenious methods of mathematical logic, sent shockwaves through the intellectual world, challenging long-held assumptions about the completeness and consistency of formal axiomatic systems.

The first incompleteness theorem states that in any consistent formal system that is sufficiently powerful to encode arithmetic, there are statements that are true but that cannot be proven within the system. In other words, there are mathematical truths that are beyond the reach of the system's axioms and rules of inference, no matter how rigorously defined or exhaustively applied.

This was a stunning revelation, because it meant that even in a system as seemingly solid and unassailable as arithmetic, there are gaps and limitations that are inherent to the system itself. No matter how many axioms we add or how sophisticated our methods of proof become, there will always be true statements that remain unprovable within the confines of the system.

Gödel's second incompleteness theorem goes even further, showing that a consistent formal system cannot prove its own consistency. In other words, if a system is powerful enough to encode arithmetic, it cannot use its own methods to demonstrate that it is free of contradictions. This means that the consistency of a system like arithmetic is inherently uncertain and can only be established from outside the system, using methods that go beyond its own rules and axioms.

The implications of Gödel's theorems are profound and far-reaching, extending well beyond the domain of pure mathematics. They have influenced fields as diverse as philosophy, computer science, and even physics, challenging our understanding of the nature of truth, knowledge, and the limits of formal reasoning.

In the realm of philosophy, Gödel's theorems have been interpreted as a blow to the logicist program, which sought to reduce all of mathematics to a set of purely logical principles. If even arithmetic is incomplete and its consistency cannot be proven from within, then the dream of a complete and consistent logical foundation for all of mathematics appears to be unattainable.

In computer science, Gödel's theorems have close connections to the work of Turing and Church on the limits of computation. Turing's proof of the undecidability of the halting problem, for example, can be seen as a specific instance of Gödel's first incompleteness theorem, showing that there are problems that are beyond the reach of any computational procedure. Similarly, the Church-Turing thesis, which asserts the equivalence of various models of computation, can be seen as a kind of consistency result that is analogous to Gödel's second theorem.

Even in physics, Gödel's ideas have found surprising applications. In the 1970s, the physicist Roger Penrose used Gödel's theorems to argue that the human mind cannot be fully explained by computational processes, since our ability to recognize mathematical truths appears to exceed the capabilities of any formal system. While this argument remains controversial, it highlights the enduring relevance of Gödel's ideas to questions about the nature of intelligence and consciousness.

As we grapple with the implications of Gödel's incompleteness theorems, we are forced to confront the limits not just of computation, but of our very ability to capture truth and knowledge within formal systems. We must recognize that even our most rigorous and carefully constructed intellectual edifices are inherently incomplete, and that there are always truths that lie beyond their grasp.

At the same time, Gödel's theorems do not negate the power and importance of formal systems and axiomatic reasoning. They simply remind us that these tools, as valuable as they are, have inherent limitations that we must acknowledge and work within. They encourage us to embrace a kind of intellectual humility, recognizing that our understanding of the world is always partial and provisional, and that there are mysteries and paradoxes that may forever elude our grasp.

In the end, Gödel's incompleteness theorems stand as a testament to the enduring mystery and complexity of the mathematical universe, and to the indomitable human spirit that drives us to explore its depths and push against its boundaries. They remind us that even as we strive to build ever more powerful and sophisticated formal systems, we must always remain humble in the face of the vast ocean of truth that lies beyond our reach, and open to the possibility of new discoveries and revelations that may shake the very foundations of our understanding.

CHAPTER 8
THE DOMINO PROBLEM

In our journey through the realm of unsolvable problems and the limits of computation, we have encountered a variety of puzzles and paradoxes that challenge our intuitions and push the boundaries of what is knowable and computable. From the halting problem to Gödel's incompleteness theorems, these problems have revealed deep truths about the nature of mathematics, logic, and computation, and have inspired new avenues of research and discovery.

In this chapter, we turn our attention to a problem that is deceptively simple in its formulation, yet remarkably complex in its implications. This is the domino problem, also known as the Wang tile problem, named after the mathematician and logician Hao Wang who first posed it in 1961.

The domino problem asks whether it is possible to tile an infinite plane using a finite set of tile types, such that no two adjacent tiles are of the same type, and the tiling pattern never repeats. More formally, we are given a set of square tiles, each of which has a color on each of its four edges. We are asked to determine whether there exists a way to arrange these tiles on an infinite grid, such that the colors on adjacent edges match, and no finite pattern of tiles is ever repeated.

At first glance, this problem may seem like a mere puzzle, a kind of mathematical game with little relevance to the wider world of computation and complexity theory. However, as we shall see, the domino problem is in fact a profound and far-reaching question that touches on some of the deepest issues in theoretical computer science and artificial intelligence.

To understand the significance of the domino problem, we must first consider its computational complexity. In 1966, Robert Berger proved that the problem of determining whether a given set of Wang tiles can tile the plane is undecidable in general. This means that there is no algorithm that can take a set of tiles as input and always correctly determine whether or not they can tile the plane.

Berger's proof was a remarkable achievement, as it showed that the domino problem is not just difficult, but fundamentally unsolvable by any computational means. It established a deep connection between the problem of tiling and the concept of undecidability, which had previously been studied in the context of logic and mathematics.

The undecidability of the domino problem has far-reaching implications for the theory of computation and the limits of what can be achieved by algorithms and machines. It shows that there are certain problems that are inherently beyond the reach of any computational procedure, no matter how powerful or sophisticated.

Moreover, the domino problem has found surprising applications in fields as diverse as computer graphics and physics. In computer graphics, Wang tiles have been used to generate aperiodic textures and patterns that can be used to create realistic-looking surfaces and backgrounds. By carefully designing sets of tiles that can tile the plane aperiodically, graphics researchers have been able to create rich and detailed visual environments that mimic the complexity and variety of the natural world.

In physics, the domino problem has been studied in the context of quasicrystals and aperiodic tilings. Quasicrystals are materials that have a highly ordered structure, but lack the translational symmetry of traditional crystals. They exhibit stunning and intricate patterns that never quite repeat, and have properties that are distinct from those of both crystalline and amorphous materials.

The discovery of quasicrystals in the 1980s challenged long-held assumptions about the nature of matter and the possible arrangements of atoms in solid materials. It showed that the seemingly simple rules of tiling and symmetry can give rise to structures of incredible complexity and beauty, and opened up new avenues for the study of materials science and condensed matter physics.

As we reflect on the significance of the domino problem and its place in the pantheon of unsolvable problems, we are reminded once again of the deep and enduring mysteries that lie at the heart of computation and mathematics. Even seemingly simple recreational puzzles like dominoes arranged on a checkerboard can lead to profundities about the boundaries of human knowledge.

The domino problem shows us that creativity and playfulness can unlock insights about the foundations of math and computer science. By tackling whimsical challenges, thinkers like Wang Hao demonstrated how recreational games connect to formal logic and computability. Though the domino problem is unsolvable, the journey of grappling with it advanced our comprehension of what computers can and cannot do.

Moreover, this relatively trivial challenge involving dominoes became a touchstone for foundational questions about computation. It joined the ranks of problems like the halting problem in illuminating the limits of algorithms. Its addition to the body of undecidable problems in math and computer science reminds us that we still have much to learn about the potential and limitations of computational systems.

As we explore the intricacies of the computational universe, we can draw inspiration from the domino problem's rich history. Despite its unsolvability, thinkers approached it with creativity and discerned profound truths. Like them, we can embrace the joy of mathematical discovery, finding beauty in complexity. Though some problems may be unsolvable, engaging with them expands our minds and knowledge. The domino problem exemplifies how playful curiosity can unlock new horizons for human creativity and understanding.

CHAPTER 9
THE WORD PROBLEM

As we continue our exploration of unsolvable problems and the frontiers of computability, we turn our attention to a fundamental question in the realm of abstract algebra and group theory. This is the Word Problem, a deceptively simple yet profoundly important question that has captivated mathematicians and computer scientists for decades.

At its core, the Word Problem asks whether, given a group specified by a set of generators and relations, there exists an algorithm to determine whether any two words (i.e., strings formed from the generators and their inverses) represent the same element of the group. In other words, can we always find a way to decide if two seemingly different sequences of group operations actually yield the same result?

To understand the significance of the Word Problem, we must first delve into the basics of group theory. A group is a fundamental algebraic structure that consists of a set of elements together with a binary operation that satisfies certain axioms, such as associativity, the existence of an identity element, and the existence of inverses for each element. Groups arise naturally in many areas of mathematics, from number theory and geometry to topology and analysis, and have applications in fields as diverse as physics, chemistry, and computer science.

One way to specify a group is by giving a set of generators, which are elements of the group that can be combined using the group operation to produce all other elements, along with a set of relations, which are equations that the generators must satisfy. For example, the group of integers under addition can be specified by a single generator (the number 1) and no relations, while the group of symmetries of a square can be specified by two generators (a rotation and a reflection) and one relation (the fact that performing two reflections in a row is equivalent to a rotation).

The Word Problem, then, asks whether, given a group specified in this way, we can always determine whether two words (i.e., sequences of generators and their inverses) represent the same element of the group. This is a natural question to ask, as it gets at the heart of what it means to understand a group and its structure.

However, in the 1950s, a series of groundbreaking results in mathematical In a pivotal development within logic and computability theory, it emerged that the Word Problem is indeed insurmountable for specific groups. That is to say, for these groups, there is no conceivable algorithm capable of unerringly discerning whether two distinct words symbolize the same group element.

This groundbreaking revelation was brought to light through the work of mathematicians Pyotr Novikov and William Boone. Each, through their independent research, established that the Word Problem defies resolution for certain finitely presented groups—those characterized by a limited set of generators and relations. The cornerstone of their proofs was the intricate interplay between group theory and the halting problem associated with Turing machines, a topic previously explored.

Specifically, Novikov and Boone showed how to construct a finitely presented group that encodes the behavior of a Turing machine in such a way that the question of whether two words represent the same element of the group is equivalent to the question of whether the Turing machine halts on a given input. Since the halting problem is undecidable, this implies that the Word Problem for this group is also undecidable. The ingenuity of their approach lies in the clever mapping between the abstract realm of group theory and the concrete computational model of Turing machines, thereby transferring the unsolvability of the halting problem to the Word Problem.

The unsolvability of the Word Problem has far-reaching implications for the study of groups and their algorithmic properties. It shows that there are fundamental limits to what we can compute and decide about groups, even when they are specified in a seemingly simple and concrete way. This realization challenges our understanding of what it means to fully comprehend the structure and behavior of a group, as there may always be questions that cannot be answered algorithmically. Furthermore, it highlights the inherent complexity that can arise from the combination of even basic mathematical objects and operations, reminding us of the depth and subtlety of abstract algebra.

The Word Problem also intersects with numerous other domains in mathematics and computer science, encompassing topology and geometry as well as cryptography and complexity theory. Take, for instance, the Higman embedding theorem. This pivotal theorem posits that every group with a recursive presentation can be embedded into a finitely presented group. The proof of this theorem is deeply intertwined with the unsolvability of the Word Problem.

In the realm of cryptography, the complexity inherent in the Word Problem for some groups serves as the foundation for devising secure communication protocols and constructing one-way functions. The underlying strategy involves selecting a group where the Word Problem is presumed to be computationally intractable. This complexity acts as a safeguard, rendering it improbable for an unauthorized interceptor to efficiently determine the solution and compromise the communication.

CHAPTER 10
THE HALTING PROBLEM

We must now inevitably confront one of the most famous and profound challenges in the history of computer science: the Halting Problem. This problem, first introduced by Alan Turing in his seminal 1936 paper "On Computable Numbers, with an Application to the Entscheidungsproblem," has become a cornerstone of theoretical computer science and a powerful lens through which to understand the nature of computation itself.

At its core, the Halting Problem asks a deceptively simple question: Is there a way to create an algorithm that can determine, for any given program and input, whether the program will eventually stop running (or "halt") or whether it will continue to run forever without halting? In other words, can we find a general procedure that can predict the behavior of any program before actually running it?

Turing's answer to this question was a resounding no. Using a brilliant and ingenious argument based on the concept of self-reference and the paradoxes of logic, Turing proved that no such algorithm can exist for all possible program-input pairs. There will always be some programs that are so complex, so intricate, and so unpredictable that it is fundamentally impossible to determine their halting behavior without actually running them and seeing what happens.

To understand the significance of this result, we must first consider the context in which Turing was working. In the early 20th century, the foundations of mathematics were undergoing a profound crisis, as paradoxes and inconsistencies began to emerge in the heart of set theory and logic. Mathematicians and philosophers were grappling with deep questions about the nature of proof, the limits of formal systems, and the possibility of a complete and consistent axiomatization of mathematics.

Against this backdrop, Turing's work on computability and the Entscheidungsproblem (the "decision problem" of determining whether a given mathematical statement is provable within a formal system) took on a new urgency and significance. By showing that the Halting Problem is unsolvable, Turing not only demonstrated the limitations of computation, but also shed new light on the nature of mathematical truth and the boundaries of what can be known and proven.

The proof of the Halting Problem's unsolvability is a masterpiece of logical reasoning and a testament to Turing's genius. The key insight is to construct a program that refers to itself in a paradoxical way, creating a kind of "vicious circle" that confounds any attempt to predict its behavior.

Specifically, Turing imagined a hypothetical program called the "Halting Oracle" that could solve the Halting Problem for any given program and input. He then constructed a second program, which we might call the "Turing Paradox Program," that works as follows: It takes any program as input, and then runs the Halting Oracle on that program and its own source code. If the Oracle determines that the input program would halt, the Turing Paradox Program enters an infinite loop and runs forever. If the

THE UNSOLVABLE PROBLEM

Oracle determines that the input program would run forever, the Turing Paradox Program halts immediately.

Now, what happens if we feed the Turing Paradox Program to itself as input? If the Halting Oracle determines that the Turing Paradox Program would halt on its own source code, then by definition, the program must enter an infinite loop and run forever. But if the Oracle determines that the program would run forever, then by definition, it must halt immediately. Either way, we arrive at a contradiction, a logical impossibility that cannot be resolved.

This contradiction proves that our initial assumption - the existence of a Halting Oracle that could solve the Halting Problem for any program and input - must be false. No such Oracle can exist, and the Halting Problem is therefore unsolvable.

The implications of this result are profound and far-reaching, extending well beyond the realm of pure mathematics and logic. In the field of computer science, the Halting Problem has become a fundamental limit on what can be computed and what can be automated. It shows that there are certain problems that are inherently undecidable, no matter how powerful our computers become or how clever our algorithms are.

This has practical consequences for software development and debugging. It means that there can never be a perfect, general-purpose tool for detecting infinite loops or other halting errors in programs. While we can certainly develop heuristics and techniques for identifying common types of errors, there will always be some programs that slip through the cracks, whose behavior is simply too complex and unpredictable to be analyzed in advance.

More broadly, the Halting Problem has become a key touchstone in the philosophy of mind and the debate over the nature of intelligence and consciousness. Some thinkers, such as the mathematician Roger Penrose, have argued that the human mind is not bound by the same limitations as formal systems and algorithms, and that our ability to solve problems and arrive at insights that are fundamentally uncomputable is evidence of a non-algorithmic, perhaps even quantum-mechanical, aspect to consciousness.

Others, such as the philosopher Daniel Dennett, have pushed back against this view, arguing that the human mind is ultimately a product of physical processes and computational mechanisms, and that the appearance of non-algorithmic insight is an illusion born of the complexity and opacity of our cognitive processes.

Regardless of where one stands on this debate, the Halting Problem reminds us of the fundamental mystery and complexity of the mind, and the way in which even the most basic questions about the nature of thought and computation can lead us to deep and unresolved philosophical quandaries.

The Halting Problem continues to be a crucial concept in modern-day computer science, with implications for various fields and applications. Here are some examples of how the Halting Problem manifests in our daily lives:

Software development: The Halting Problem reminds us that there is no foolproof way to guarantee that a program will always run correctly and terminate without encountering errors. Debuggers and testing tools can help identify common bugs, but they cannot guarantee that a program is completely free of halting errors.

Security vulnerabilities: The Halting Problem can be exploited by attackers to create programs that can halt or crash systems unexpectedly. For example, a malicious program could be designed to enter an infinite loop or consume all available resources, leading to a denial-of-service attack.

Artificial intelligence: The Halting Problem has implications for the development of artificial intelligence (AI). While AI systems are becoming increasingly sophisticated, there is no guarantee that they will always make decisions that lead to desired outcomes or terminate within a reasonable timeframe.

Resource management: The Halting Problem highlights the importance of efficient resource management in computing systems. Programs that run indefinitely or consume excessive resources can lead to system slowdowns and crashes.

Game theory and decision-making: The Halting Problem can be applied to game theory and decision-making problems. For example, in a game of chess, it is impossible to determine in advance whether a particular strategy will lead to a win or a loss, as the game can potentially continue indefinitely.

These examples demonstrate how the Halting Problem is a fundamental concept that has real-world implications in various fields. Understanding the limitations of computation and the unsolvability of certain problems is essential for developing robust, reliable, and secure systems.

The Halting Problem also raises intriguing philosophical questions about the nature of intelligence and consciousness. Is it possible for a machine to truly understand and solve problems that are fundamentally unsolvable for algorithms? These questions continue to inspire debate and research in the fields of artificial intelligence and philosophy of mind.

CHAPTER 11

THE POST CORRESPONDENCE PROBLEM

As we continue our exploration of the uncomputable and the undecidable, we encounter yet another problem that has captured the imagination of mathematicians and computer scientists for generations: the Post Correspondence Problem, or PCP for short. This problem, first introduced by the mathematician and logician Emil Post in 1946, has become a fundamental part of the theory of computation, with deep connections to automata theory, formal languages, and the foundations of mathematics.

The Post Correspondence Problem is a deceptively simple yet profoundly challenging question about the nature of strings and the limits of algorithmic decision-making. It asks us to consider two lists of strings, and to determine whether there is a way to construct a new string by alternating and concatenating elements from each list, such that the resulting strings are identical.

THE UNSOLVABLE PROBLEM

More formally, the problem can be stated as follows: Given two lists of strings $A = (a_1, a_2, ..., a_n)$ and $B = (b_1, b_2, ..., b_n)$, is there a sequence of indices $i_1, i_2, ..., i_k$ such that $a_{i_1} + a_{i_2} + ... + a_{i_k} = b_{i_1} + b_{i_2} + ... + b_{i_k}$, where "+" denotes string concatenation?

To make this more concrete, let's consider a simple example. Suppose we have two lists of strings:

A = ("ab", "c", "ab") B = ("a", "bc", "abc")

In this case, we can construct a solution to the PCP by choosing the indices 1, 3, 2, which yields:

$a_{i_1} + a_{i_3} + a_{i_2}$ = "ab" + "ab" + "c" = "ababc" $b_{i_1} + b_{i_3} + b_{i_2}$ = "a" + "abc" + "bc" = "ababc"

Thus, for this particular instance of the problem, there is indeed a solution, and we can answer "yes" to the question posed by the PCP.

However, the true significance of the PCP lies not in the individual instances that can be solved, but rather in the question of whether there exists a general algorithm that can decide, for any given pair of lists A and B, whether a solution exists. In other words, can we find a foolproof procedure that can take any PCP instance as input and always correctly determine whether it has a solution or not?

Surprisingly, the answer to this question is no. In a series of groundbreaking results in the 1960s and 1970s, researchers in theoretical computer science and mathematical logic showed that the PCP is, in fact, undecidable. This means that there is no algorithm that can solve the PCP for all possible inputs, no matter how much time and computing power we have at our disposal.

The undecidability of the PCP has far-reaching implications for our understanding of computation and the limits of what can be automated. It shows that there are certain problems in mathematics and computer science that are inherently unsolvable, not because we lack the intelligence or the resources to solve them, but because they are fundamentally beyond the reach of any algorithmic procedure.

To prove the undecidability of the PCP, researchers had to develop sophisticated techniques in mathematical logic and the theory of computation. One key insight was the use of reductions, which allowed them to show that the PCP is at least as hard as other known undecidable problems, such as the Halting Problem that we encountered in the previous chapter.

The basic idea behind a reduction is to show that if we could solve the PCP, then we could also solve another problem that we know to be undecidable. This establishes a kind of "chain of undecidability" that connects the PCP to some of the deepest and most fundamental questions in logic and computation.

For example, one famous reduction shows that the PCP is at least as hard as the problem of determining whether a given Turing machine (a simple abstract model of computation) will halt on a given input. Since the Halting Problem is undecidable, this implies that the PCP must also be undecidable, as any algorithm that could solve the PCP could be used to solve the Halting Problem as well.

The undecidability of the PCP has important implications for many areas of computer science and mathematics. In the field of formal languages, for example, the PCP is closely related to the concept of context-free grammars, which are used to describe the structure and syntax of programming languages and other formal systems. The undecidability of the PCP implies that there are certain questions about context-free grammars that cannot be answered by any algorithm, no matter how sophisticated.

In the field of automated theorem proving, the PCP has been used to show the limitations of certain proof systems and decision procedures. By encoding instances of the PCP as logical formulas, researchers have been able to demonstrate that there are certain types of mathematical statements that cannot be proven or disproven by any automated means, even in principle.

Beyond its technical implications, the PCP also has a certain philosophical and conceptual significance. It reminds us that even the most basic and elementary questions about strings and sequences can lead us to the very boundaries of what is knowable and computable. It shows that there are certain truths in mathematics that are forever beyond our grasp, not because they are too complex or too abstract, but because they are inherently undecidable.

In this sense, the PCP is a kind of conceptual mirror, reflecting back to us the limits and the paradoxes of our own minds. It challenges us to confront the mysteries of language and meaning, and to grapple with the fundamental nature of computation and reasoning.

As we ponder the implications of the PCP and its place in the pantheon of undecidable problems, we are reminded once again of the power and the beauty of the mathematical imagination. We see how even the most simple and innocuous questions can lead us to the very frontiers of human knowledge, and how the pursuit of understanding can take us to places we never dreamed possible.

In the end, the Post Correspondence Problem is more than just a curiosity or a technical challenge. It is a testament to the enduring wonder and mystery of the mathematical universe, and to the limitless possibilities of the human mind. It invites us to embrace the unknown and the undecidable, and to find joy and meaning in the pursuit of knowledge, even in the face of the most daunting and intractable problems.

As we continue our journey through the realm of the uncomputable and the undecidable, let us carry with us the lessons and the insights of the PCP, and let us approach each new challenge with the same sense of curiosity, creativity, and intellectual humility that has driven the greatest minds in science and mathematics throughout history. For it is only by pushing the boundaries of what is possible that we can truly begin to understand the nature of computation and the limits of our own understanding.

CHAPTER 12
BRIDGING THE GAP BETWEEN LOGIC AND REALITY

Throughout our exploration of the limits of computation and the boundaries of logical reasoning, we've stumbled upon a recurring theme: the disconnect between the abstract world of logical models and the concrete reality of everyday life. This disconnect is at the heart of what we call the verification problem, which asks us to consider how we can ensure that the truths we derive through logical reasoning actually hold up in the real world.

To understand this problem, let's consider a simple example. Imagine we have a logical statement that says:

For all people, if a person is a responsible adult, then they will not engage in risky behaviors.

In the language of logic, we might write this as:

\\(\\forall x (R(x) \\rightarrow \\neg B(x)) \\)

Here, $R(x)$ means "x is a responsible adult," and $B(x)$ means "x engages in risky behaviors."

From a purely logical standpoint, this statement makes perfect sense. If we define "responsible adult" as someone who doesn't engage in risky behaviors, then the statement $\forall x (R(x) \rightarrow \neg B(x))$ must be true by definition.

But when we try to apply this logic to the real world, things get messy. To actually verify whether this statement holds true in reality, we'd need to observe the behavior of every single person who we consider to be a responsible adult. If we find even one responsible adult who engages in a risky behavior, then our logical statement is proven false in the real world, no matter how much sense it makes in the abstract.

This discrepancy between logical truth and empirical reality has big implications across many fields, from philosophy and mathematics to computer science and artificial intelligence. It raises deep questions about the nature of knowledge, the limitations of formal systems, and how abstract models relate to the concrete world around us.

In philosophy, this issue has been a central concern of the empiricist tradition, which emphasizes the importance of sensory experience and observational evidence in acquiring knowledge. Empiricists argue that the truth of a statement can only be determined through direct observation or experimentation, and that logic alone isn't enough to establish the truth of claims about the world.

On the other hand, the rationalist tradition in philosophy holds that certain truths can be known through reason alone, independent of sensory experience. Rationalists believe that the human mind can grasp abstract concepts and principles that go beyond the physical world, and that these concepts can be used to derive necessary truths about reality.

THE UNSOLVABLE PROBLEM

In the 20th century, a philosophical movement known as logical positivism tried to bridge the gap between empiricism and rationalism. The logical positivists sought to establish a firm foundation for science and mathematics based on the principles of logic and empirical verification. They argued that the only meaningful statements were those that could be verified through empirical observation or logical proof.

However, the logical positivist project ran into its own set of problems. The principle of verification, which was central to their philosophy, turned out to be self-defeating. The statement "a claim is only meaningful if it can be empirically verified or logically proven" cannot itself be empirically verified or logically proven. Moreover, the positivists' attempts to reduce all knowledge to basic sensory experiences and logical axioms led to issues of circularity and infinite regress.

The lesson of the verification problem is that the relationship between logic and empiricism, between abstract models and concrete realities, is complex and often fraught with difficulties. While logic is a powerful tool for organizing and analyzing our knowledge about the world, it cannot, by itself, guarantee the truth of our beliefs or the accuracy of our predictions about reality.

At the same time, empirical observation and experimentation, while crucial for grounding our theories in reality, are themselves shaped by our prior assumptions, our measurement tools, and our conceptual frameworks. Our observations can never provide a completely neutral or objective view of the world.

The challenge, then, is to find a balance between pure logic and raw empiricism, to develop a nuanced understanding of how abstract reasoning and concrete experience interact and inform each other. This is a challenge that has occupied some of the greatest thinkers in the history of science and philosophy.

In the realm of computer science and artificial intelligence, the verification problem is particularly pressing. As we develop increasingly sophisticated algorithms and models for reasoning and decision-making, we need to ensure that these models are not just logically consistent, but also empirically valid and practically useful.

This is especially important in the field of machine learning, where the goal is often to build models that can generalize from limited data to make predictions about new, unseen cases. Here, the verification problem becomes a question of validating the performance of our models on real-world data, and making sure they are not simply memorizing noise or detecting spurious correlations.

Computer scientists and AI researchers have developed various methods for model validation and testing, such as cross-validation, bootstrapping, adversarial testing, and formal verification. These techniques aim to provide a more rigorous way of assessing the empirical adequacy of our models and identifying potential sources of bias or error.

Despite these advanced tools and methods, the verification problem remains a fundamental challenge for AI and for the broader project of building intelligent systems that can reason about the world. As we continue to push the boundaries of machine learning and automated reasoning, we must remain aware of the limitations of pure logic and the need for continuous empirical validation.

In the end, the verification problem teaches us that the search for knowledge and understanding is an ongoing process, and that the relationship between abstract models and concrete realities is always evolving. As we navigate the complex landscape of science, technology, and philosophy, we must stay open to new ideas and approaches while also maintaining a commitment to empirical rigor and healthy skepticism.

The verification problem is not merely a technical challenge, but a deeper philosophical question that gets to the heart of what it means to be human. It reminds us of the inherent uncertainty and incompleteness of our knowledge, and of the constant need for inquiry, experimentation, and revision in the face of an ever-expanding universe of possibilities.

As we continue our journey through the frontiers of computability, logic, and empiricism, let us embrace this challenge with open minds, creativity, and humility, knowing that the process of asking questions and seeking answers is as important as the conclusions we reach. It is only by engaging with the deepest and most difficult problems of our time that we can hope to build a more rational, empirical, and enlightened understanding of ourselves and the world around us.

CHAPTER 13
UNSOLVABLE PROBLEMS IN EVERYDAY LIFE

As we've explored the depths of unsolvable problems in the abstract realms of mathematics and computer science, it's easy to think that these concepts are far removed from our everyday experiences. However, the truth is that we encounter unsolvable problems in various aspects of our lives, from the personal and social to the political and economic. While these problems may not always involve complex mathematical formulas, they share the same fundamental characteristics of incompleteness, undecidability, and uncertainty.

One of the most familiar examples of an unsolvable problem in everyday life is the challenge of making perfect decisions. Whether we're choosing a career path, a life partner, or even what to have for dinner, we're often faced with a multitude of options and a limited amount of information. Even when we try to weigh the pros and cons and consider all the possible outcomes, there's no guarantee that we'll make the "right" choice, because the future is inherently uncertain and unpredictable.

THE UNSOLVABLE PROBLEM

This problem is compounded by the fact that our decisions are often influenced by a wide range of factors, from our personal preferences and biases to the social and cultural norms that shape our worldviews. What may seem like a perfectly rational choice to one person may be completely unthinkable to another, based on their unique experiences, values, and beliefs.

In the realm of social and political life, unsolvable problems take on an even greater significance. Consider the challenge of creating a perfectly just and equitable society, one in which every individual has equal opportunities and resources, and where discrimination and oppression are eliminated. While this is a noble and important goal, it's also one that has proven to be elusive throughout human history, despite the best efforts of activists, reformers, and revolutionaries.

The reasons for this are complex and multifaceted, but they stem in part from the fact that social and political systems are inherently complex and dynamic, with countless variables and interactions that are difficult to predict or control. Even when we try to address one problem, such as inequality or discrimination, we may inadvertently create new problems or exacerbate existing ones, leading to a kind of whack-a-mole game of social change.

Moreover, the very definition of what constitutes a just and equitable society is itself a matter of debate and disagreement, with different individuals and groups holding different values, priorities, and visions for the future. What may seem like a perfectly reasonable and necessary reform to one group may be seen as a threat or an infringement on the rights and freedoms of another.

Another example of an unsolvable problem in everyday life is the challenge of achieving perfect health and well-being. While modern medicine and public health have made incredible strides in preventing and treating disease, prolonging life, and promoting healthy behaviors, the fact remains that illness, injury, and death are an inevitable part of the human experience.

Even with the most advanced medical technologies and the most comprehensive healthcare systems, there will always be limits to what we can achieve in terms of health and longevity. Some diseases and conditions may be incurable or untreatable, some risk factors may be unavoidable or uncontrollable, and some individuals may simply be more susceptible to illness or injury than others.

Moreover, the very definition of health and well-being is itself a complex and multifaceted concept, encompassing not just physical health but also mental, emotional, and social well-being. What may be considered healthy or desirable for one person may be completely inappropriate or unattainable for another, based on their unique circumstances, preferences, and values.

In the realm of personal relationships and emotions, unsolvable problems take on a particularly poignant and intimate character. Consider the challenge of finding and maintaining perfect love, happiness, and fulfillment in our lives. While these are all things that most of us strive for, the truth is that they are often elusive and fleeting, subject to the vagaries of chance, circumstance, and human nature.

Even in the closest and most loving relationships, there will always be moments of conflict, misunderstanding, and disappointment, as well as joy, connection, and growth. No matter how much we care for someone or how compatible we may seem, there will always be differences and challenges that we must navigate and negotiate, often without any clear or easy solutions.

THE UNSOLVABLE PROBLEM

Moreover, our own emotions and desires are themselves complex and sometimes contradictory, shaped by a lifetime of experiences, beliefs, and conditioning. What may bring us happiness and fulfillment at one moment may leave us feeling empty or dissatisfied the next, and what may seem like a source of meaning and purpose in our lives may eventually lose its luster or relevance.

Ultimately, the lesson of unsolvable problems in everyday life is that the human experience is inherently complex, uncertain, and open-ended, and that there will always be limits to what we can know, predict, or control. Whether we're grappling with personal decisions, social and political challenges, health and well-being, or the mysteries of love and emotion, we must learn to embrace the inherent incompleteness and ambiguity of the world around us.

This doesn't mean that we should give up on trying to solve problems or make positive changes in our lives and in the world. On the contrary, the recognition of unsolvable problems can be a source of inspiration and motivation, pushing us to think creatively, act compassionately, and strive for progress and growth in the face of uncertainty and adversity.

But it does mean that we must approach these challenges with a sense of humility, openness, and resilience, recognizing that there will always be more to learn, more to discover, and more to grapple with as we navigate the complexities of the human experience. It means being willing to embrace the unknown and the unknowable, to find beauty and meaning in the imperfections and contradictions of life, and to continue the ongoing quest for understanding and connection in a world that is always in flux.

As we move forward in an age of rapid technological change and global interconnectedness, the lessons of unsolvable problems in everyday life will only become more relevant and pressing. They remind us that even as we strive to create a more just, equitable, and fulfilling world, we must remain grounded in the realities of the human condition, with all its messiness, diversity, and unpredictability.

By embracing these challenges with courage, compassion, and curiosity, we can continue to grow and learn as individuals and as a society, finding new ways to navigate the unsolvable problems of everyday life with grace, resilience, and hope. And in doing so, we can create a future that is not just more technologically advanced, but also more humanly rich and meaningful, one that honors the full complexity and potential of the human experience.

CHAPTER 14

THE PRISONER'S DILEMMA

One of the most fascinating and perplexing unsolvable problems in the realm of social science and game theory is the Prisoner's Dilemma. This thought experiment, first formulated by mathematicians Merrill Flood and Melvin Dresher in the 1950s, presents a scenario where two individuals must choose between cooperating with each other or betraying one another, without knowing what the other will do.

The setup is as follows: two suspects are arrested and separately interrogated by the police. The police have insufficient evidence to convict either suspect, so they offer each a deal. If one suspect confesses and the other remains silent, the confessor will go free, and the silent suspect will receive a heavy sentence. If both suspects confess, they will both receive a reduced sentence. If both remain silent, they will both receive a light sentence for a minor charge.

The Prisoner's Dilemma presents a fascinating thought experiment that reveals the paradoxical nature of rational self-interest. The dilemma arises from the fact that, regardless of what the other suspect does, each individual's best option is to confess. If the other suspect remains silent, confessing will result in going free. If the other suspect confesses, confessing will result in a reduced sentence rather than a heavy one. However, if both suspects confess, they will both end up with a worse outcome than if they had both remained silent.

This seemingly simple scenario illuminates the complex interplay between individual and collective rationality. Game theorists have extensively analyzed the Prisoner's Dilemma using mathematical models and computer simulations. These analyses demonstrate that betraying the other player produces the optimal outcome from a self-interested perspective. Yet if both players betray each other, they each face a worse outcome than mutual cooperation. This creates an intriguing tension between rational choices at the individual level versus optimal outcomes at the group level.

The Prisoner's Dilemma has profound implications in diverse fields including economics, political science, biology, and computer science. Evolutionary biologists, for instance, have applied the model to study the evolution of cooperation. The paradox helps explain how altruistic behaviors, which benefit the group at the expense of individuals, can evolve through natural selection. Insights from the Prisoner's Dilemma have shaped game theory, social psychology, ethics, and theories of human nature. This seemingly straightforward hypothetical scenario continues to reveal deep truths about the complex dynamics of self-interest, competition, trust, and cooperation.

Thought experiment: Imagine you and a friend are the suspects in this scenario. You cannot communicate with each other, and you must make your decision independently. What would you choose, and why? How would your decision change if you knew that you would be in this situation with your friend repeatedly, rather than just once?

THE UNSOLVABLE PROBLEM

The Prisoner's Dilemma has been studied extensively by game theorists, psychologists, and evolutionary biologists, among others. It has been used to model a wide range of real-world situations, from arms races and advertising campaigns to climate change negotiations and public goods provision.

One key insight from this research is that cooperation can indeed emerge and be sustained, even in situations that resemble the Prisoner's Dilemma. This can happen through mechanisms such as reciprocity, reputation, and the evolution of social norms. When individuals interact repeatedly, they have an incentive to cooperate, as they can punish betrayal and reward cooperation over time. When individuals can observe and share information about each other's behavior, they can develop reputations for being trustworthy or untrustworthy, which can shape their future interactions. And when societies develop norms and institutions that promote and enforce cooperation, individuals can learn to cooperate even in one-shot, anonymous encounters.

However, the Prisoner's Dilemma also highlights the fragility of cooperation and the constant threat of defection. In many real-world situations, the temptation to cheat or free-ride on the cooperation of others can be strong, especially when the stakes are high or the consequences of defection are not immediately apparent. Sustaining cooperation often requires active effort, communication, and the alignment of individual and collective interests.

As you reflect on the Prisoner's Dilemma, consider the following questions:

1. In what situations in your own life have you faced a dilemma similar to the Prisoner's Dilemma? How did you navigate the tension between your individual interests and the potential benefits of cooperation?

2. How do social norms and institutions in your community promote or hinder cooperation? Can you think of examples where cooperation has broken down due to the temptation to defect?

3. In an increasingly interconnected and globalized world, how can we foster cooperation and trust across boundaries of culture, nationality, and identity? What role can individuals, organizations, and governments play in this process?

By grappling with these questions and exploring the complex dynamics of cooperation and defection, we can gain a deeper understanding of the unsolvable problems that shape our social world, and the potential for human ingenuity and collaboration to overcome them.

CHAPTER 15
THE PARADOX OF CHOICE

In our daily lives, we are constantly faced with choices - from the mundane, like what to have for breakfast, to the monumental, like what career to pursue or who to spend our lives with. The abundance of options available to us in modern society is often seen as a blessing, a sign of freedom and prosperity. However, as psychologist Barry Schwartz argues in his book "The Paradox of Choice," having too many options can actually lead to anxiety, dissatisfaction, and even paralysis.

The core idea behind the paradox of choice is that while having some choice is undoubtedly good, having too much choice can overwhelm our cognitive capacities and lead to suboptimal decision-making. When faced with a plethora of options, we may struggle to weigh the relative costs and benefits of each one, leading to indecision or a nagging sense of regret about the path not taken.

In the case of Sheena Iyengar and Mark Lepper's jam study, the findings illustrate a profound psychological effect now widely known as the paradox of choice. This phenomenon suggests that while an abundance of options might seem appealing, it can actually lead to decision fatigue, overwhelm, and a reduced likelihood of making a decision at all. The impact of this phenomenon extends far beyond simple choices in grocery stores—it touches on nearly every aspect of modern life, where consumers face a dizzying array of choices from what smartphone to buy, to what shows to watch on streaming platforms.

Further exploration of the paradox of choice reveals that when individuals are faced with many options, they often experience anxiety and a higher level of regret after making a decision. This regret isn't necessarily because the choice they made was inferior, but because of the awareness of all the other options they had to reject. Consequently, this awareness can lead to lower overall satisfaction. This counterintuitive outcome challenges the conventional wisdom that more choice leads to greater happiness.

Research in behavioral economics and psychology continues to uncover how the paradox of choice impacts our satisfaction and decision-making processes. For example, studies have shown that an overload of choices can lead to poorer quality decisions and a decrease in the likelihood of engaging in a decision-making process at all. This is especially pertinent in complex decisions like selecting healthcare plans or retirement investment options. In these high-stakes environments, too many choices can lead to procrastination or the selection of options that are not optimized for the individual's long-term benefit.

The implications of this understanding are significant for marketers, product designers, and policymakers. By limiting choices to a more manageable selection, companies can potentially increase customer satisfaction and sales. For policymakers, simplifying choices in public services, such as health insurance and retirement plans, could lead to better outcomes for citizens.

Moreover, understanding the paradox of choice can also lead to better personal decision-making strategies. By voluntarily limiting one's options and focusing on what truly aligns with one's needs and values, individuals can reduce stress and make more satisfying decisions. This approach requires a conscious effort to recognize when choice is becoming counterproductive and taking steps to simplify the decision-making environment.

In conclusion, the paradox of choice reshapes our understanding of optimal decision-making in a world saturated with options. It challenges the traditional models of economic rationality and opens up new avenues for research into human behavior. This phenomenon has implications across various disciplines and industries, offering a lens through which we can reevaluate how we present choices in our personal and professional lives. As we continue to navigate an increasingly complex world, understanding and managing the paradox of choice will be crucial in enhancing our ability to make decisions that are not only rational but also conducive to our overall well-being.

Consider the following thought experiment: You are planning a vacation and have narrowed it down to two options - a beach resort in the Caribbean or a cultural tour of Europe. Both options have their pros and cons, and you find yourself torn between them. How do you make your decision?

According to the rational choice model, you would carefully weigh the costs and benefits of each option, considering factors such as price, duration, activities, and personal preferences, and choose the one that provides the greatest overall value or utility. However, the paradox of choice suggests that this process may not be so straightforward.

You may find yourself overwhelmed by the sheer number of sub-options within each category - which Caribbean island? Which European cities? What type of accommodation? What activities to prioritize? You may also be swayed by emotional factors, such as the opinions of friends and family, the allure of social media posts, or a fear of missing out on the "perfect" experience.

Moreover, even after making a decision, you may find yourself plagued by doubts and regrets, wondering if you made the right choice or if the other option would have been better. This "grass is greener" mentality can lead to chronic dissatisfaction and a sense that the chosen option is never quite good enough.

So how can we navigate the paradox of choice and make decisions that align with our values and preferences? One approach is to embrace the concept of "satisficing" rather than maximizing. Satisficing, a term coined by economist Herbert Simon, means settling for a choice that is "good enough" rather than endlessly searching for the perfect option. By setting clear criteria for what constitutes an acceptable choice and being willing to accept trade-offs, we can reduce the cognitive burden of decision-making and avoid the pitfalls of endless deliberation.

Another strategy is to cultivate mindfulness and self-awareness in our decision-making processes. By tuning into our emotional responses and underlying motivations, we can gain clarity about what truly matters to us and make choices that align with our authentic preferences and values. This may involve practices such as journaling, meditation, or seeking feedback from trusted advisors.

Finally, we can work to create choice environments that are more conducive to effective decision-making. This may involve simplifying options, providing clear and relevant information, and designing interfaces that guide users towards optimal choices. In the realm of public policy, this approach is known as "choice architecture" and has been applied to domains ranging from retirement savings to organ donation.

By grappling with these questions and exploring the paradoxical nature of choice, we can develop a more nuanced understanding of the unsolvable problems that shape our lives and the ways in which we can respond to them with wisdom, resilience, and grace.

CHAPTER 16
THE SORITES PARADOX

Language is a powerful tool for communication, reasoning, and understanding. It allows us to express complex ideas, share knowledge, and coordinate our actions with others. However, language is also inherently fuzzy and ambiguous, full of borderline cases and gray areas that resist clear-cut categorization. This fuzziness lies at the heart of many unsolvable problems in philosophy, linguistics, and cognitive science.

One of the most famous examples of the fuzziness of language is the Sorites Paradox, also known as the paradox of the heap. The paradox goes like this: imagine a heap of sand. If you remove one grain of sand from the heap, it will still be a heap. If you remove another grain, it will still be a heap. If you continue this process, at what point does the heap cease to be a heap? Is there a clear boundary between a heap and a non-heap?

The Sorites Paradox arises from the vagueness of the concept of a "heap." While we may have a general sense of what constitutes a heap, there is no precise definition or cut-off point. This vagueness is not limited to the concept of a heap, but applies to many other terms and categories in natural language, such as "tall," "bald," "red," or "chair."

Here's a thought experiment to illustrate the paradox: imagine a spectrum of colors ranging from pure red to pure orange. At what point does red become orange? Is there a single wavelength of light that marks the boundary between the two colors? Or is there a range of wavelengths that are borderline cases, neither clearly red nor clearly orange?

The Sorites Paradox poses challenges for theories of meaning and truth in natural language. If the meaning of a term like "heap" or "red" is inherently fuzzy and admits of borderline cases, how can we assign truth values to statements involving those terms? Is the statement "this is a heap of sand" true or false if the pile of sand is right on the borderline of what counts as a heap?

One approach to resolving the Sorites Paradox is to embrace the idea of degrees of truth or fuzzy logic. Rather than assigning a binary true/false value to a statement, fuzzy logic allows for statements to be partially true or partially false, depending on where they fall on the spectrum of vagueness. For example, the statement "this person is tall" might be 70% true for someone who is 6'2", but only 30% true for someone who is 5'10".

Another approach is to recognize that the meaning of terms in natural language is often context-dependent and subject to social conventions and norms. What counts as a "heap" or a "tall person" may vary depending on the specific circumstances and the shared understanding of the language community. By acknowledging the role of context and convention in shaping meaning, we can develop more nuanced and flexible approaches to language use and interpretation.

This exploration into the fuzziness of language underscores the intricate challenges that both humans and artificial intelligence systems face in communication. As AI continues to advance, the development of algorithms capable of navigating the subtleties of human language remains a pivotal area of research. This task is particularly daunting due to the inherent ambiguities and nuances of linguistic expression, which often rely on context and cultural background for meaning.

The Sorites Paradox, for instance, demonstrates the limits of binary logic when applied to categories that don't have strict boundaries, such as defining when a heap of sand becomes a heap as grains are removed one by one. This type of vagueness poses significant challenges for AI, particularly in natural language processing (NLP) where the goal is to parse, understand, and generate human-like text based on incomplete and often imprecise data.

In response to these challenges, researchers in AI and NLP have developed various models and techniques aimed at better handling linguistic fuzziness. Techniques such as deep learning, which can process large datasets to identify patterns and nuances in language use, have significantly advanced the field. However, these technologies are not without their limitations. While they can mimic certain linguistic abilities, understanding and replicating the depth of human language, with all its irregularities and contextual requirements, remains a work in progress.

Moreover, the issues raised by the fuzziness of language also highlight a broader philosophical question about the nature of knowledge and communication. Formal logic and precise definitions offer clarity and are invaluable in fields where precision is paramount, such as mathematics and computer science. Yet, they often fall short in capturing the full spectrum of human expression and thought, which are fluid and dynamically shaped by social interactions and cultural contexts.

Engaging with the philosophical dimensions of language and its paradoxes not only deepens our understanding of linguistic structures but also enriches AI research. By integrating insights from linguistics, cognitive science, and philosophy, AI developers can create more sophisticated systems that better emulate human-like understanding and responsiveness.

The pursuit of solving the unsolvable problems of language fuzziness is not merely a technical challenge; it is a window into the human condition. As we strive to enhance AI's linguistic capabilities, we concurrently unravel layers of human cognition and social interaction. This endeavor does not only aim to achieve technological advancements but also fosters a deeper comprehension of what it means to communicate and understand in a human way.

Thus, while the problems of language vagueness and ambiguity may resist definitive solutions, they propel ongoing research and philosophical inquiry. Each step forward in this field not only improves AI's capabilities but also enriches our insights into the complex interplay between language, thought, and society. As AI becomes increasingly integrated into our daily lives, understanding and addressing these linguistic challenges will be crucial for developing systems that are not only technically proficient but also culturally and socially attuned.

CHAPTER 17

THE POST CORRESPONDENCE PROBLEM

In the realm of theoretical computer science and formal language theory, the Post Correspondence Problem (PCP) stands as a seminal example of an undecidable problem. Introduced by the renowned mathematician and logician Emil Post in 1946, the PCP elegantly encapsulates the inherent limitations of computational decision-making and has far-reaching implications for our understanding of the nature of algorithms and the boundaries of solvability.

At its core, the Post Correspondence Problem is a deceptively simple question about strings and their concatenation. Given a set of pairs of strings, the challenge is to determine whether there exists a sequence of indices such that the concatenation of the first elements of the selected pairs is identical to the concatenation of the second elements. More formally, let us consider a set of pairs of strings $\{(u\_1, v\_1), (u\_2, v\_2), ..., (u\_n, v\_n)\}$, where u_i and v_i are strings over some alphabet. The PCP asks whether there exists a sequence of indices $i\_1, i\_2, ..., i\_k$ such that

$u_{i_1} + u_{i_2} + \ldots + u_{i_k} = v_{i_1} + v_{i_2} + \ldots + v_{i_k}$, where "+" denotes string concatenation.

At first glance, the PCP might appear to be a straightforward string matching problem, akin to those commonly encountered in text processing and information retrieval. However, the true nature of the PCP is far more profound and complex. In a groundbreaking result, Post demonstrated that the PCP is, in fact, undecidable. This means that there is no algorithm, no matter how sophisticated or powerful, that can solve the PCP for all possible instances. In other words, there is no general procedure that can take any set of string pairs as input and determine, in a finite number of steps, whether a matching sequence of indices exists.

The undecidability of the PCP has far-reaching implications for our understanding of the limits of computation and the boundaries of algorithmic decision-making. It reveals that there are certain problems, even those that can be clearly and concisely stated, that lie beyond the reach of any computational procedure. The PCP belongs to a class of problems known as "undecidable" or "non-computable," which includes other famous examples such as the Halting Problem and Gödel's Incompleteness Theorems.

To appreciate the significance of the PCP, it is essential to understand the concept of decidability and its role in the theory of computation. In simplest terms, a problem is considered decidable if there exists an algorithm that can solve it in a finite number of steps for all possible inputs. Such an algorithm is often referred to as a decision procedure, as it effectively decides whether a given input satisfies a particular property or belongs to a specific set. The concept of decidability is closely tied to the notion of computability, which deals with the fundamental limits of what can be computed by algorithms and Turing machines.

The theory of computation, as developed by pioneers like Alan Turing, Alonzo Church, and Emil Post himself, provides a rigorous mathematical framework for studying the nature of decidability and computability. At the heart of this theory lies the concept of the Turing machine, an abstract model of computation that captures the essential capabilities and limitations of algorithms. Turing machines consist of a tape divided into cells, a read-write head that can move along the tape, and a finite set of states that govern the machine's behavior. By encoding problems as inputs to Turing machines and studying their behavior, researchers can gain deep insights into the inherent complexity and solvability of computational tasks.

The undecidability of the Post Correspondence Problem, like that of the Halting Problem, stems from the inherent limitations of Turing machines and the nature of computation itself. The proof of the PCP's undecidability relies on a technique known as reduction, which allows researchers to show that if a problem is decidable, then another known undecidable problem would also be decidable, leading to a contradiction. In the case of the PCP, the reduction typically involves encoding the Halting Problem or a similar undecidable problem into an instance of the PCP. By demonstrating that a solution to the PCP would imply a solution to the Halting Problem, which is known to be impossible, the undecidability of the PCP is established.

The undecidability of the PCP has profound implications for various areas of computer science and mathematics. In the field of formal language theory, the PCP is closely related to the study of context-free languages and their properties. The PCP can be seen as a way of testing whether two context-free languages, generated by the first and second elements of the string pairs, have a non-empty intersection. The undecidability of the PCP implies that there is no algorithm that can determine, in general, whether two context-free languages intersect, a result known as the undecidability of the context-free language intersection problem.

THE UNSOLVABLE PROBLEM

In the area of automated theorem proving and program verification, the PCP has important implications for the limits of what can be achieved by computational methods. Many problems in these fields, such as determining whether a given logical formula is satisfiable or whether a program meets its specification, can be reduced to instances of the PCP or similar undecidable problems. The undecidability of the PCP suggests that there are inherent limitations to the power of automated reasoning systems and that certain problems in logic and program analysis may be fundamentally unsolvable.

The PCP also has connections to the field of cryptography and the study of one-way functions. A one-way function is a mathematical function that is easy to compute but difficult to invert, meaning that given an output, it is computationally infeasible to find an input that produces that output. One-way functions are essential building blocks for many cryptographic protocols, such as public-key encryption and digital signatures. The undecidability of the PCP can be used to construct one-way functions and to prove the security of certain cryptographic schemes. By reducing an instance of the PCP to a cryptographic problem, researchers can show that solving the cryptographic problem would imply solving the PCP, which is impossible, thereby establishing the security of the cryptographic construction.

Beyond its technical implications, the Post Correspondence Problem also serves as a powerful reminder of the fundamental limits of human knowledge and the inherent complexity of the universe. The undecidability of the PCP demonstrates that there are certain truths, even within the realm of pure mathematics and abstract symbol manipulation, that are forever beyond the reach of any computational procedure. It highlights the fact that the world is not always reducible to simple, algorithmic solutions and that there are problems that defy our best efforts to tame them with the tools of logic and computation.

This realization has profound philosophical implications, challenging our understanding of the nature of knowledge, truth, and the role of the human mind in the universe. The undecidability of problems like the PCP suggests that there may be fundamental limits to what we can know and understand, even in principle. It raises questions about the relationship between abstract mathematical concepts and the physical world, and about the extent to which our intelligence and creativity are bound by the same limitations as our computational models.

At the same time, the study of undecidable problems like the PCP also serves as a testament to the power and ingenuity of the human intellect. By pushing the boundaries of what is computable and exploring the frontiers of decidability, researchers in theoretical computer science and mathematics are expanding our understanding of the nature of information, complexity, and the limits of knowledge. They are developing new techniques and frameworks for grappling with the inherent intractability of certain problems, and finding ways to circumvent or mitigate the effects of undecidability in practical settings.

Moreover, the PCP and other undecidable problems serve as a source of inspiration and wonder, inviting us to contemplate the deep mysteries of the universe and the nature of the human mind. They remind us that even in the realm of pure abstraction, there are questions that may forever elude our grasp, and that the pursuit of knowledge is an ongoing, open-ended journey with no fixed destination.

The Post Correspondence Problem stands as a powerful symbol of the limits of computation and the boundaries of decidability. Its undecidability has far-reaching implications for our understanding of the nature of algorithms, the complexity of formal languages, and the fundamental limits of knowledge. By exploring the PCP and other undecidable problems, we gain a deeper appreciation for the richness and subtlety of the abstract world of computation, and a renewed sense of humility in the face of the vast, uncharted territories of the mathematical universe. As we continue to push the boundaries of what is computable and to grapple with the inherent complexity of the world around us, the lessons of the PCP will continue to guide and inspire us, reminding us of the enduring power and mystery of the human mind.

CHAPTER 18
THE SPECTRUM PROBLEM

In the realm of mathematical logic and model theory, the Spectrum Problem stands as a formidable challenge that has captivated researchers for decades. This problem delves into the intricate relationship between logical theories and the sizes of their finite models, revealing the profound complexities and subtle nuances that underlie the foundations of mathematical reasoning.

At its core, the Spectrum Problem seeks to determine the possible cardinalities of finite models for a given logical theory. In other words, it asks: given a set of axioms and inference rules that define a particular logical system, what are the possible sizes of the structures that satisfy those axioms? This seemingly simple question has far-reaching implications for our understanding of the expressive power of logical languages, the nature of mathematical truth, and the limits of what can be formally proven or disproven.

THE UNSOLVABLE PROBLEM

To appreciate the significance of the Spectrum Problem, it is essential to understand the concept of a model in logical theory. A model is a mathematical structure that provides an interpretation for the symbols and formulas of a logical language, making them "true" in a specific context. For example, in the language of first-order logic, a model consists of a non-empty set (called the universe or domain) along with interpretations for the constant symbols, function symbols, and relation symbols of the language. A formula in first-order logic is said to be true in a model if it holds under the given interpretation, and a theory is a set of formulas that are all true in a particular class of models.

The study of models and their properties lies at the heart of model theory, a branch of mathematical logic that investigates the connections between formal languages and the structures that satisfy them. Model theory has deep connections to various areas of mathematics, including algebra, topology, and number theory, and has found applications in fields as diverse as computer science, linguistics, and philosophy.

The Spectrum Problem arises naturally in the context of model theory, as it probes the fundamental question of what kinds of structures can be described or axiomatized by a given logical language. In particular, it focuses on finite models, which are structures with a finite universe or domain. Finite models are of particular interest in many areas of mathematics and computer science, as they often represent discrete, combinatorial objects that arise in practical applications.

The complexity of the Spectrum Problem stems from the fact that the answer can vary widely depending on the specific logical framework being considered and the particular conditions or restrictions placed on the models. In some cases, the problem may be relatively straightforward, with a clear characterization of the possible sizes of finite models. In other cases, the problem may be extremely difficult or even undecidable, meaning that there is no algorithmic procedure that can determine the answer in general.

One of the earliest and most celebrated results in the study of the Spectrum Problem is the Löwenheim-Skolem Theorem, named after the logicians Leopold Löwenheim and Thoralf Skolem. This theorem states that if a first-order theory has any infinite model, then it has models of all infinite cardinalities. In other words, if a set of first-order axioms can be satisfied by an infinite structure, then there are models of that theory of every possible infinite size.

The Löwenheim-Skolem Theorem has profound implications for the expressive power of first-order logic and the nature of mathematical truth. It shows that first-order logic, despite its apparent richness and versatility, cannot capture certain fundamental properties of mathematical structures, such as their size or cardinality. This limitation has led to the development of more powerful logical frameworks, such as second-order logic and infinitary logics, which can express a wider range of mathematical concepts and properties.

However, the increased expressive power of these stronger logics often comes at the cost of increased complexity and decreased decidability. In many cases, the Spectrum Problem for these logics becomes even more challenging, with fewer general results and more intricate dependencies on the specific axioms and conditions being considered.

One particularly notable example of the complexity of the Spectrum Problem arises in the context of finite model theory, which focuses on the properties of logical theories that have only finite models. In this setting, the Spectrum Problem asks which sets of natural numbers can be realized as the set of sizes of finite models of a given theory. This version of the problem has deep connections to computer science and computational complexity theory, as it relates to the expressive power of various logical languages and the complexity of certain algorithmic problems.

In the realm of finite model theory, the Spectrum Problem has been shown to be closely related to the theory of computational complexity classes, such as P, NP, and PSPACE. In particular, certain versions of the Spectrum Problem have been proven to be complete for these complexity classes, meaning that they are among the hardest problems within those classes and can be used to characterize the complexity of other problems.

For example, the Spectrum Problem for first-order logic with a single binary relation symbol has been shown to be NEXPTIME-complete, implying that it is among the hardest problems that can be solved by a nondeterministic Turing machine in exponential time. This result highlights the intricate connections between logical theories, computational complexity, and the fundamental limits of algorithmic problem-solving.

The Spectrum Problem also has important implications for the philosophy of mathematics and the nature of mathematical knowledge. It raises questions about the objectivity and universality of mathematical truth, and the extent to which our understanding of mathematical structures is shaped by the logical frameworks we use to describe them.

In particular, the Spectrum Problem highlights the inherent limitations of any fixed logical system in capturing the full richness and diversity of mathematical structures. It suggests that our knowledge of mathematics is always relative to the specific axioms and inference rules we adopt, and that there may be fundamental aspects of mathematical reality that are forever beyond the reach of any particular formal theory.

This realization has led some philosophers and logicians to embrace a more pluralistic and open-ended view of mathematics, one that recognizes the multiplicity of possible logical frameworks and the inherent incompleteness of any single system. From this perspective, the Spectrum

Problem is not just a technical challenge to be overcome, but a profound reminder of the inexhaustible mystery and complexity of the mathematical universe.

Despite its complexity and philosophical implications, the Spectrum Problem remains an active area of research in mathematical logic and theoretical computer science. Researchers continue to investigate the spectra of various logical theories, seeking to characterize the possible sizes of their finite models and to uncover new connections between logic, computation, and mathematics.

Some of the most exciting developments in this area have come from the application of sophisticated mathematical techniques, such as model-theoretic forcing, stability theory, and classification theory, to the study of the Spectrum Problem. These tools have enabled researchers to prove powerful results about the structure and complexity of logical theories, and to uncover deep connections between seemingly disparate areas of mathematics.

At the same time, the Spectrum Problem has also inspired the development of new computational methods and algorithms for analyzing logical theories and their models. These include techniques for building finite models of theories, for testing the satisfiability of logical formulas, and for automatically generating proofs and counterexamples.

As we continue to explore the frontiers of logic and computation, the Spectrum Problem will undoubtedly remain a central and enduring challenge. Its complexity and depth reflect the fundamental nature of mathematical reasoning itself, and its resolution will likely require the combined efforts of logicians, mathematicians, computer scientists, and philosophers.

But beyond its technical significance, the Spectrum Problem also serves as a powerful reminder of the beauty and mystery of the abstract realm of logic and mathematics. It invites us to contemplate the nature of truth and knowledge, to question our assumptions about the foundations of reasoning, and to marvel at the intricacy and elegance of the formal systems we use to describe the world.

In this sense, the Spectrum Problem is not just a problem to be solved, but a gateway to a deeper understanding of the nature of thought itself. By grappling with its complexities and exploring its implications, we not only expand the frontiers of logic and mathematics, but also enrich our appreciation of the power and limitations of the human mind.

CHAPTER 19
RICHARD'S PARADOX

In the realm of mathematical logic and the foundations of mathematics, Richard's Paradox stands as a perplexing and thought-provoking example of the inherent limitations of formal systems. This paradox, first introduced by the French mathematician Jules Richard in 1905, delves into the intricate relationship between language, definability, and the nature of mathematical objects, revealing the profound challenges that arise when attempting to provide a complete and consistent description of the mathematical universe.

At its core, Richard's Paradox is concerned with the concept of definability in mathematics, particularly as it relates to the description of real numbers. The paradox arises from the interplay between the expressive power of language and the inherent self-referential nature of certain mathematical statements, leading to a puzzling contradiction that challenges our understanding of the very foundations of mathematics.

To understand the essence of Richard's Paradox, let us first consider the notion of definability in the context of real numbers. In mathematics, a real number is considered definable if it can be uniquely specified or described

THE UNSOLVABLE PROBLEM

using a finite combination of words, symbols, and logical operations. For example, the number π (pi) can be defined as the ratio of a circle's circumference to its diameter, while the number e (Euler's number) can be defined as the base of the natural logarithm.

However, the set of definable real numbers is itself a countable set, meaning that it can be put into one-to-one correspondence with the natural numbers (1, 2, 3, ...). This is because there are only a finite number of words and symbols available in any given language, and thus only a countable number of possible combinations that can be used to define real numbers.

Richard's Paradox arises when we consider the following self-referential definition of a real number:

"Let R be the real number whose nth decimal digit is 1 if the nth definable real number has a 0 in its nth decimal place, and 0 otherwise."

At first glance, this definition may seem innocuous, as it appears to specify a unique real number R based on the properties of other definable real numbers. However, upon closer examination, a paradox emerges.

If R is itself a definable real number, then it must appear somewhere in the enumeration of definable real numbers, say at position k. But by its very definition, the kth decimal digit of R depends on the kth decimal digit of the kth definable real number, which is R itself. This creates a circular reference, as the definition of R depends on the properties of R, leading to a logical contradiction.

On the other hand, if R is not a definable real number, then it should not appear in the enumeration of definable real numbers. However, we have just provided a precise definition of R using a finite combination of words and symbols, which suggests that R should, in fact, be definable.

This paradox highlights the inherent limitations and challenges that arise when attempting to provide a complete and consistent description of the mathematical universe using language and formal systems. It demonstrates that self-referential statements, even those that appear to be well-defined and logically coherent, can lead to contradictions and paradoxes that cannot be easily resolved within the standard frameworks of mathematics.

The implications of Richard's Paradox extend far beyond the realm of real numbers and definability. It is part of a broader class of paradoxes in mathematical logic, alongside notable examples such as Russell's Paradox and the Liar's Paradox, that expose the fundamental tensions between language, truth, and formal systems.

These paradoxes challenge the notion of a complete and consistent mathematical universe that can be fully captured and described by any single formal system. They suggest that there may be inherent limitations to the expressive power of language and logic, and that certain mathematical truths may be inherently paradoxical or unsolvable within the confines of standard mathematical frameworks.

The discovery of Richard's Paradox and other related paradoxes had a profound impact on the development of mathematical logic and the foundations of mathematics in the early 20th century. It contributed to the realization that the naive and intuitive approaches to set theory and logic that had prevailed up to that point were insufficient to provide a solid and consistent foundation for mathematics.

In response to these paradoxes, mathematicians and logicians embarked on a rigorous program to formalize and axiomatize the foundations of mathematics, leading to the development of formal systems such as Zermelo-Fraenkel set theory (ZF) and first-order logic. These formal systems sought to provide a consistent and reliable framework for mathematical reasoning, while carefully circumscribing the scope and limits of mathematical definability and truth.

However, even with these formal systems in place, the specter of incompleteness and undecidability continued to haunt the foundations of mathematics. The groundbreaking work of Kurt Gödel in the 1930s, particularly his famous incompleteness theorems, showed that any consistent formal system powerful enough to encode arithmetic must necessarily contain statements that are true but unprovable within the system itself.

Gödel's incompleteness theorems, along with the earlier paradoxes of Russell and Richard, fundamentally challenged the notion of a complete and decidable mathematical universe. They revealed that there are inherent limitations to the power of formal systems and that the pursuit of a perfect and all-encompassing mathematical framework may be an unattainable goal.

Despite these limitations, the study of paradoxes and the foundations of mathematics continues to be a rich and active area of research. Mathematicians, logicians, and philosophers grapple with the implications of these paradoxes and seek to develop new approaches and frameworks for understanding the nature of mathematical truth and the limits of formal systems.

One important area of investigation is the study of non-standard models and alternative logical frameworks that can accommodate and make sense of paradoxical statements and self-referential structures. These approaches often involve relaxing or modifying the standard axioms and rules of inference, allowing for a more expansive and inclusive view of mathematical truth.

Another important line of inquiry is the exploration of the connections between paradoxes, computability theory, and the limits of algorithmic reasoning. Many of the most famous undecidable problems in computer science, such as the halting problem and the Entscheidungsproblem, can be seen as manifestations of the same underlying limitations of formal systems that give rise to paradoxes like Richard's Paradox.

The study of computational complexity theory and the classification of problems into tractable and intractable classes has also shed light on the inherent difficulties and limitations of mathematical problem-solving. The discovery of NP-complete problems and the P versus NP question have revealed the existence of a vast landscape of mathematical and computational challenges that may resist efficient algorithmic solutions.

In the realm of philosophy, Richard's Paradox and related paradoxes have inspired deep reflections on the nature of language, truth, and meaning. They have challenged traditional conceptions of logic and rationality, and have led to the development of new philosophical frameworks, such as paraconsistent logic and dialetheism, that seek to make sense of contradictory and paradoxical statements.

Moreover, the paradoxes of self-reference and definability have also found resonance in fields beyond mathematics and philosophy, such as linguistics, psychology, and the arts. The notion of self-reference and the blurring of boundaries between language and reality have been explored in works of literature, such as in the writings of Jorge Luis Borges and Douglas Hofstadter, and in the visual arts, such as in the self-referential drawings of M.C. Escher.

As we continue to grapple with the implications of Richard's Paradox and the limits of mathematical definability, we are reminded of the enduring mystery and complexity of the abstract realm of mathematics. We are challenged to confront the inherent limitations of our linguistic and logical tools, and to seek new ways of understanding and navigating the paradoxical and self-referential aspects of mathematical truth.

At the same time, the paradoxes of self-reference also invite us to marvel at the richness and creativity of human thought, and to appreciate the ways in which language and meaning can transcend the boundaries of formal systems. They remind us that the pursuit of mathematical knowledge is not just a quest for certainty and consistency, but also an exploration of the enigmatic and the paradoxical, an embrace of the irreducible complexity and beauty of the mathematical universe.

In this sense, Richard's Paradox and the challenges it poses are not just obstacles to be overcome, but also invitations to a deeper engagement with the nature of mathematics and the limits of human understanding. By grappling with these paradoxes and pushing the boundaries of our logical and linguistic frameworks, we not only advance the frontiers of mathematical knowledge but also enrich our appreciation of the profound and mysterious aspects of mathematical truth.

CHAPTER 20

THE KOLMOGOROV COMPLEXITY

In the realm of information theory and theoretical computer science, the concept of Kolmogorov complexity has emerged as a fundamental measure of the inherent complexity and randomness of data objects. Developed independently by Ray Solomonoff, Andrey Kolmogorov, and Gregory Chaitin in the 1960s, Kolmogorov complexity provides a rigorous mathematical framework for quantifying the amount of information contained in a string of symbols, and for exploring the limits of algorithmic compressibility and description.

At its core, Kolmogorov complexity is concerned with the shortest possible description of a given data object, such as a string of bits, in a fixed universal description language. The Kolmogorov complexity of a string is defined as the length of the shortest program that can generate that string when run on a universal Turing machine, a theoretical model of computation that can simulate any other computable process.

Intuitively, the Kolmogorov complexity of a string can be thought of as a measure of its inherent algorithmic content or information density. Strings that exhibit a high degree of regularity, pattern, or structure will have low Kolmogorov complexity, as they can be described by relatively short programs that exploit these regularities. On the other hand, strings that are highly irregular, random, or unstructured will have high Kolmogorov complexity, as they require longer and more complex programs to generate them.

The study of Kolmogorov complexity has deep connections to a wide range of areas in theoretical computer science, mathematics, and physics. It provides a unifying framework for understanding the nature of information, randomness, and complexity, and has led to significant advances in fields such as algorithmic information theory, data compression, machine learning, and the foundations of probability and statistics.

However, despite its conceptual elegance and powerful applications, Kolmogorov complexity is known to be non-computable or uncomputable. This means that there is no algorithm or Turing machine that can compute the Kolmogorov complexity of an arbitrary string in a finite amount of time. In other words, the problem of determining the shortest possible description of a given string is itself an unsolvable problem, one that lies beyond the reach of any computational procedure.

The non-computability of Kolmogorov complexity has profound implications for our understanding of the limits of algorithmic reasoning and the fundamental boundaries of what can be effectively described or compressed by computational means. It reveals that there are certain aspects of information and complexity that are inherently irreducible and uncomputable, and that no matter how powerful our computational tools become, there will always be certain problems and questions that remain beyond their grasp.

To understand the non-computability of Kolmogorov complexity, it is helpful to consider some of the key mathematical ideas and techniques that underlie its definition and properties. At the heart of Kolmogorov complexity lies the concept of a universal Turing machine, a theoretical model of computation that can simulate any other computable process or algorithm.

A Turing machine consists of a tape divided into cells, each of which can hold a symbol from a finite alphabet, and a read-write head that can move along the tape, reading and writing symbols according to a fixed set of rules or instructions. The machine operates by executing a sequence of steps, each of which involves reading a symbol from the tape, writing a symbol to the tape, moving the head left or right, and transitioning to a new state based on the current state and the symbol read.

By encoding programs and data as strings of symbols on the tape, a Turing machine can perform any computable task, from simple arithmetic operations to complex simulations and optimizations. The universal Turing machine takes this idea one step further, by allowing the description of any other Turing machine to be encoded on its tape, along with the input data for that machine. In this way, the universal Turing machine can simulate the behavior of any other computable process, making it a powerful tool for studying the nature of computation and information.

The Kolmogorov complexity of a string is defined in terms of the length of the shortest program that can generate that string when run on a universal Turing machine. More formally, let U be a fixed universal Turing machine, and let x be a finite binary string. The Kolmogorov complexity of x with respect to U, denoted $K\_U(x)$, is the length of the shortest program p such that $U(p) = x$, where $U(p)$ denotes the output of U when run on input p.

While the choice of universal Turing machine U may affect the specific value of $K\_U(x)$ for a given string x, it can be shown that the Kolmogorov

THE UNSOLVABLE PROBLEM

complexity is invariant up to an additive constant that depends only on U. This means that the Kolmogorov complexity provides a robust and objective measure of the inherent information content of a string, independent of the specific computational model or encoding scheme used.

However, the non-computability of Kolmogorov complexity arises from the fact that there is no algorithm or Turing machine that can compute $K\_U(x)$ for an arbitrary string x. This can be shown using a simple counting argument, based on the fact that there are far more strings of a given length than there are short programs that can generate them.

More specifically, let n be a positive integer, and consider the set of all binary strings of length n. There are 2^n such strings, each of which can be viewed as a potential output of a program running on the universal Turing machine U. However, there are only $2^{(n-1)}$ possible programs of length less than n, since each such program can be encoded as a binary string of length at most n-1.

This means that there must be at least one string x of length n such that $K\_U(x) \geq n$, since otherwise there would be more strings of length n than there are programs of length less than n to generate them. In other words, for any fixed universal Turing machine U and any positive integer n, there must be at least one "incompressible" string of length n, whose Kolmogorov complexity is at least as large as its length.

The existence of incompressible strings is a fundamental consequence of the non-computability of Kolmogorov complexity, and has deep implications for our understanding of the nature of information and randomness. It suggests that there are certain strings that are inherently complex and unstructured, and that cannot be effectively compressed or described by any short program.

Moreover, the non-computability of Kolmogorov complexity implies that there is no algorithm or Turing machine that can solve the "Kolmogorov complexity problem" of determining the shortest program that generates a given string. This is because any such algorithm would have to be able to compute $K\_U(x)$ for an arbitrary string x, which is impossible by the counting argument above.

The non-computability of Kolmogorov complexity has far-reaching implications for a wide range of areas in theoretical computer science and mathematics. In the field of algorithmic information theory, it is closely related to the concept of algorithmic randomness, which seeks to define and study the properties of random objects in terms of their Kolmogorov complexity.

A string is considered algorithmically random if its Kolmogorov complexity is close to its length, meaning that it cannot be effectively compressed or described by any significantly shorter program. The study of algorithmic randomness has led to significant advances in our understanding of the nature of randomness and its role in computation, cryptography, and other areas.

In the field of data compression, the non-computability of Kolmogorov complexity sets fundamental limits on the effectiveness of compression algorithms and the achievable compression ratios for certain types of data. It suggests that there are certain files or data sets that are inherently incompressible, and that no lossless compression scheme can achieve a compression ratio better than a certain threshold determined by the Kolmogorov complexity of the data.

In the field of machine learning and artificial intelligence, the non-computability of Kolmogorov complexity has implications for the design and analysis of learning algorithms and the limits of what can be learned from data. It suggests that there are certain patterns or regularities in data that may be difficult or impossible to detect or exploit using computable methods, and that the performance of learning algorithms may be fundamentally limited by the inherent complexity of the data being analyzed.

Beyond its technical implications, the non-computability of Kolmogorov complexity also raises deep philosophical questions about the nature of information, complexity, and the limits of human knowledge. It challenges our intuitive notions of simplicity and complexity, and suggests that there may be fundamental aspects of reality that are beyond the reach of algorithmic description or understanding.

At the same time, the study of Kolmogorov complexity and its non-computability has also led to significant advances in our understanding of the creative and expressive power of computation. It has inspired new approaches to the design and analysis of algorithms, and has led to the development of powerful techniques for quantifying and harnessing the information content of data in fields such as data compression, machine learning, and cryptography.

As we continue to explore the frontiers of theoretical computer science and navigate the complexities of the information age, the insights and challenges posed by the non-computability of Kolmogorov complexity will undoubtedly continue to shape our understanding of the nature of computation and the limits of algorithmic reasoning. It reminds us of the enduring mystery and beauty of the abstract realm of information, and invites us to embrace the unknown and the uncomputable as we seek to push the boundaries of human knowledge and creativity.

In this sense, the non-computability of Kolmogorov complexity is not just a technical result or a limitation to be overcome, but a profound reflection on the nature of human inquiry and the endless possibilities of the computational universe. It challenges us to think deeply about the nature of information and complexity, and to approach the study of computation with a sense of humility, curiosity, and wonder.

As we continue on this journey of discovery, the non-computability of Kolmogorov complexity will undoubtedly remain a source of inspiration and puzzlement, reminding us of the enduring importance of theoretical computer science and the fundamental questions it seeks to answer. By grappling with the complexities and paradoxes of Kolmogorov complexity and its non-computability, we not only advance our understanding of the foundations of computation, but also enrich our appreciation of the rich and mysterious tapestry of information that underlies the world around us.

CHAPTER 21
THE BUSY BEAVER PROBLEM

The Busy Beaver problem stands as a fascinating and enigmatic challenge that probes the very limits of what can be computed and predicted by algorithmic means. Introduced by the mathematician Tibor Radó in 1962, the Busy Beaver problem is a deceptively simple question that asks: what is the maximum number of steps that a Turing machine with a given number of states and symbols can take before halting, when started on an empty tape?

Despite its seemingly innocuous formulation, the Busy Beaver problem has captured the imagination of computer scientists and mathematicians for decades, and has become a cornerstone of the theory of computability and the study of the limits of algorithmic reasoning. It is a problem that lies at the intersection of computer science, mathematics, and philosophy, and that raises deep questions about the nature of computation, the limits of mathematical knowledge, and the fundamental boundaries of what can be predicted or computed by any means.

At its core, the Busy Beaver problem is concerned with the behavior of Turing machines, the abstract mathematical models of computation that form the foundation of modern computer science. A Turing machine is a theoretical device that consists of an infinite tape divided into cells, each of which can hold a symbol from a finite alphabet, and a read-write head that can move along the tape, reading and writing symbols according to a fixed set of rules or states.

The number of states and symbols in a Turing machine can vary, and each combination of states and symbols defines a different class of machines with its own computational power and complexity. The Busy Beaver problem asks, for each such class of machines, what is the maximum number of steps that any machine in that class can take before halting, when started on an empty tape?

More formally, let $\Sigma(n,m)$ denote the set of all Turing machines with n states and m symbols, and let $S(M)$ denote the number of steps taken by a machine M before halting, when started on an empty tape. The Busy Beaver function, denoted $BB(n,m)$, is defined as the maximum value of $S(M)$ over all machines M in $\Sigma(n,m)$. In other words, $BB(n,m)$ represents the maximum number of steps that any n-state, m-symbol Turing machine can take before halting, when started on an empty tape.

The Busy Beaver problem asks, for each pair of positive integers n and m, what is the value of $BB(n,m)$? In other words, it seeks to determine the maximum computational power or "busyness" of Turing machines with a given number of states and symbols, and to find the machines that achieve this maximum.

Despite its apparent simplicity, the Busy Beaver problem is known to be not only unsolvable, but also to grow faster than any computable function. This means that there is no algorithm or Turing machine that can compute

BB(n,m) for arbitrary values of n and m, and that the value of BB(n,m) increases so rapidly with n and m that it cannot be bounded or approximated by any computable function.

The unsolvability of the Busy Beaver problem can be demonstrated using a proof by contradiction, based on the halting problem for Turing machines. The halting problem, which asks whether a given Turing machine will halt on a given input, is known to be undecidable, meaning that there is no algorithm that can solve it for all possible inputs.

To prove that the Busy Beaver problem is unsolvable, we can assume that there exists an algorithm A that can compute BB(n,m) for any given values of n and m. We can then use A to solve the halting problem, by constructing a Turing machine M that simulates a given machine N on a given input, and keeps track of the number of steps taken by N.

If N halts on the given input, then M will also halt, and the number of steps taken by M will be equal to the number of steps taken by N. However, if N does not halt on the input, then M will continue running forever, taking more and more steps without ever halting.

Now, suppose we run A on the parameters n and m, where n is the number of states in M and m is the number of symbols used by M. If A could compute BB(n,m), then it could tell us the maximum number of steps that any n-state, m-symbol Turing machine could take before halting. But this would allow us to solve the halting problem for N, by comparing the number of steps taken by M to BB(n,m).

If the number of steps taken by M exceeds BB(n,m), then we know that N must not halt on the given input, since no n-state, m-symbol machine can take more steps than the Busy Beaver. On the other hand, if M halts within BB(n,m) steps, then we know that N must also halt on the input, since M is simulating N step-for-step.

But this contradicts the undecidability of the halting problem, which implies that no such algorithm A can exist. Therefore, the Busy Beaver problem must also be unsolvable, and there can be no algorithm that can compute BB(n,m) for arbitrary values of n and m.

The unsolvability of the Busy Beaver problem has profound implications for our understanding of the limits of computation and the fundamental boundaries of what can be predicted or computed by algorithmic means. It shows that there are certain properties of Turing machines and computational processes that are inherently uncomputable, and that cannot be determined or predicted by any finite means.

Moreover, the Busy Beaver problem is known to grow faster than any computable function, meaning that the value of BB(n,m) increases so rapidly with n and m that it cannot be bounded or approximated by any algorithm or mathematical formula. This is a consequence of the fact that the Busy Beaver function is not computable, and that it encodes a type of information or complexity that is fundamentally irreducible and uncomputable.

To illustrate the immense growth rate of the Busy Beaver function, consider the following examples. For n = 1 and m = 2, it is known that BB(1,2) = 1, meaning that the busiest 1-state, 2-symbol Turing machine takes only one step before halting. However, for n = 2 and m = 2, the value of BB(2,2) is already 6, and for n = 3 and m = 2, the value of BB(3,2) is at least 21, and possibly much larger.

As n and m increase, the value of BB(n,m) grows so rapidly that it quickly becomes unimaginably large. For example, it is known that BB(5,2) is at least 47,176,870, and that BB(6,2) is at least $7.4 \times 10^{36,534}$, a number so large that it cannot be written out in full using all the atoms in the observable universe.

THE UNSOLVABLE PROBLEM

The immense growth rate of the Busy Beaver function has deep implications for our understanding of the nature of computation and the limits of mathematical knowledge. It suggests that there are certain problems or questions in mathematics and computer science that are not only unsolvable, but also fundamentally irreducible and uncomputable, in the sense that they encode a type of complexity or information that cannot be captured or approximated by any finite means.

This has led some researchers to view the Busy Beaver function as a kind of "mathematical monster," a function that grows so rapidly and encodes such vast amounts of uncomputable information that it pushes the very boundaries of what can be known or understood by the human mind. In this sense, the Busy Beaver problem is not just a technical challenge or a curiosity, but a profound reflection on the nature of mathematical truth and the limits of human knowledge.

At the same time, the study of the Busy Beaver problem and its related concepts has also led to significant advances in our understanding of the nature of computation and the properties of Turing machines. It has inspired new approaches to the design and analysis of algorithms, and has led to the development of powerful techniques for proving lower bounds on the complexity of computational problems.

Moreover, the Busy Beaver problem has also found surprising connections to other areas of mathematics and theoretical computer science, such as complexity theory, algorithmic information theory, and the study of random sequences. It has been used to prove important results in these fields, and has led to new insights into the nature of randomness, complexity, and the limits of computation.

As we continue to explore the frontiers of computability theory and push the boundaries of what can be known and computed, the Busy Beaver problem will undoubtedly remain a source of fascination and inspiration for researchers and thinkers in many fields. It reminds us of the enduring mystery and beauty of the abstract realm of computation, and invites us to embrace the unknown and the uncomputable as we seek to expand the limits of human knowledge and understanding.

In this sense, the Busy Beaver problem is not just a mathematical curiosity or a technical challenge, but a profound reflection on the nature of the human mind and the endless possibilities of the computational universe. It challenges us to think deeply about the nature of information, complexity, and the limits of knowledge, and to approach the study of computation with a sense of humility, curiosity, and wonder.

CHAPTER 22

THE LIMITS OF KNOWLEDGE AND PERCEPTION

Our understanding of both past and future is intrinsically constrained. We operate largely on hypotheses and educated estimates when it comes to anticipating future events, recognizing that these forecasts, though sometimes precise, do not equate to absolute knowledge. Similarly, our grasp of historical events is broad but superficial; the fine details of everyday lives and occurrences throughout history remain largely obscure. The annals of history capture only a tiny fraction of the myriad actions, conversations, and events that have unfolded. What's more, even our perception of current events is remarkably limited. Amidst the vast flow of information and activity that surrounds us daily, we grasp only a small piece of the ongoing narrative. Thus, our episodic memory—our recollection of specific events experienced by us or reported to us—is but a narrow window into the vast expanse of human and worldly affairs.

Our knowledge of the world is also limited by our senses. We can only see, hear, smell, taste, and touch a small fraction of what is out there. A study on human cognitive processing limits, including sensory and brain processing capacities, underscores this point. According to research, our brains can only manage a finite amount of information at any given time and process this information at limited speeds.

Human cognition, a subject of extensive study in neuroscience and psychology, reveals that despite the brain's complexity and adaptability, our cognitive processing capabilities have notable limits, particularly in handling multiple pieces of information simultaneously.

George A. Miller's landmark 1956 study, "The Magical Number Seven, Plus or Minus Two," proposed that humans can hold about 7±2 pieces of information in their short-term memory at one time. This groundbreaking research into human cognitive capacity and limitations revealed that our ability to retain information over brief periods is surprisingly limited. Miller's work showed that most adults can store between 5 and 9 items in their short-term memory. This key finding shaped our understanding of short-term memory and its constraints.

Miller's paper has had an enduring influence across fields like cognitive psychology, neuroscience, and computer science. His quantification of our cognitive limits helped establish human short-term memory capacity. It also provided a concrete number for short-term memory that researchers could investigate further. Miller's revelation that people max out at remembering about 7 pieces of information simultaneously explained why we often struggle to juggle large amounts of data at once.

The speed at which information is processed also significantly affects cognitive performance. Faster processing speeds are associated with higher intelligence and enhanced problem-solving abilities. Studies on reaction times have shown that a simple response to a visual stimulus takes about 250 milliseconds, which serves as a baseline for more complex tasks that require additional cognitive operations such as integration and decision-making.

Consequently, even if we had access to all the information available, understanding everything comprehensively would be unachievable. The sheer complexity, intricacy, and vastness of the world far exceed our sensory and cognitive capabilities, ensuring that some aspects of reality will always remain beyond our reach.

To illustrate this concept, imagine a detailed, colorful illustration depicting a human figure standing before a massive library filled with books. The figure can only reach and read a few books at a time, symbolizing the limitation of human sensory and cognitive processing in comprehending the vast repository of universal knowledge. The library stretches out endlessly beyond the figure, representing the overwhelming scale of information that we can never fully grasp. This image vividly captures the concept of our limited ability to perceive and understand the complete scope of the world around us.

Despite these limitations, we can still learn a great deal about the world. We can learn about the past by studying history and archaeology. We can reconstruct fragments of ancient lives, cultures, and events. We can learn about the present by observing the world around us, taking note of patterns and changes over time. And we can learn about the future by making predictions based on our knowledge of the past and present, extrapolating trends into reasonable forecasts.

We can also learn a great deal about ourselves. We can learn about our strengths and weaknesses, our likes and dislikes, and our hopes and dreams. We can come to understand our own psychology, emotions, and cognition. We can learn about our values and beliefs, and about how we want to live our lives. Self-knowledge is a profound and ongoing process.

The process of learning is never-ending. There is always more to learn about the world and about ourselves. And the more we learn, the better equipped we are to make informed decisions and to live meaningful lives. Each answer leads to new questions and new horizons of the unknown.

While it is certainly fascinating to explore the theoretical limits of our understanding, there are practical constraints that may hinder our ability to obtain conclusive evidence for certain concepts. Theories such as dark matter, dark energy, string theory, quantum gravity, and the multiverse are among the many unsolved problems that lie at the boundaries of our current knowledge. Additionally, the nature of consciousness remains a subject of debate, with no clear consensus on its definition or origin. It is crucial to acknowledge the potential limitations of our understanding and the need for ongoing research in these areas. Despite the challenges, scientists and researchers continue to make progress towards uncovering the mysteries of the universe and pushing the boundaries of human knowledge.

String theory posits the existence of incredibly small strings, which Brian Greene has famously described as being to an atom what a tree is to the entire universe. Thomas Hertog, a prominent theoretical physicist, has further elaborated on the minuscule scale of these strings, stating that "You would need a particle accelerator as large as the solar system to probe scales that small." However, despite the daunting challenge of observing these theoretical constructs directly, there is still reason for hope.

The groundbreaking LIGO (Laser Interferometer Gravitational-Wave Observatory) detector has demonstrated an astonishing capability, detecting changes in its 4-kilometer length that are on the order of one-thousandth the size of a proton, caused by the passage of a gravitational wave. This remarkable achievement suggests that even the most elusive phenomena in the universe may eventually yield to the ingenuity and technological advancements of scientific inquiry.

The rapid progress in the field of artificial intelligence (AI), combined with the potential of quantum computing, may provide new avenues for finding evidence and explanations that have thus far eluded researchers. As the boundaries of human knowledge continue to expand, the critical question arises: will we eventually know everything there is to be known, or will there be an ongoing succession of unknowns, stretching into the infinite expanse like the endless decimal places of pi? Fortunately, humanity has been granted a significant window of time to continue this pursuit of understanding, with approximately five billion years before the Earth is engulfed by the expanding Sun, providing ample opportunity to unravel the mysteries of the universe.

CHAPTER 23

THE BOUNDARIES OF KNOWLEDGE

Here we will explore the practical boundaries of what we can know, contrasting the philosophical definition of knowledge as "justified true belief" with a more tangible, down-to-earth perspective. This practical viewpoint emphasizes our limitations in knowing the future, understanding the past, and even comprehending the fine details of present realities.

First, consider the nature of our knowledge regarding the future. It's clear that we cannot claim true knowledge of what has yet to occur. While we may make educated guesses or even accurate predictions based on current data and trends, these are not certainties but probabilities. Similarly, our grasp of the past, though broad in scope, lacks in the granular details of daily occurrences. Historical records provide us with snapshots, mere fragments of a vast and complex tapestry of human and natural history.

Turning our gaze to the present, we encounter a similar predicament. The intricate details of events unfolding around us are largely obscured, hidden

THE UNSOLVABLE PROBLEM

by the sheer complexity and volume of simultaneous activities and interactions. Thus, our episodic knowledge—that is, our knowledge of specific events and experiences—is inherently limited.

The core of our inquiry in this chapter, however, lies in exploring the limits of our understanding about the very nature of reality itself: the physical laws that govern it and the entities that play integral roles within it. We face "known unknowns" that define the current frontiers of scientific inquiry. Critical areas lacking full explanation or sufficient evidence include phenomena such as dark matter, dark energy, string theory, quantum gravity, the concept of the multiverse, and the enigma of consciousness.

These scientific mysteries underscore significant gaps in our understanding of the universe. The field of string theory, for example, challenges our fundamental perceptions of particles. Instead of being point-like dots, they are envisioned as elongated strings, the dimensions of which are incredibly small. This scale is so minute that effective experimental verification seems nearly impossible with current technology. Thomas Hertog's observation about the need for a particle accelerator as large as the solar system to probe these scales highlights the vast disparity between our theoretical ambitions and our practical capabilities.

However, technological innovations continue to push the boundaries of what is possible. The LIGO detector's success in detecting minuscule spacetime disturbances caused by gravitational waves demonstrates that even the most subtle phenomena can be observed with the right tools. This achievement not only marks a triumph in observational capability but also suggests that we may not be as far from accessing other subtle cosmic phenomena as we might think.

The integration of artificial intelligence and advancements in quantum computing further augments our potential to overcome existing barriers in scientific research. AI's capability to process and analyze vast datasets with speed and precision can uncover patterns and insights beyond human reach, while quantum computing offers the possibility of performing calculations at speeds unachievable by traditional computers. These technologies could revolutionize our approach to unsolved scientific questions, potentially accelerating the pace at which we can test theories and validate hypotheses.

This ongoing expansion of knowledge raises a interesting question: Is there a limit to what we can know? Just as pi continues to unfold its digits in an infinite progression, so too might our scientific discoveries continue to expand without end. The pursuit of knowledge, driven by insatiable human curiosity and rapid technological advancement, seems destined to continue as long as humanity exists. This quest, stretching potentially until the end of Earth's viability—when the Sun expands and engulfs our planet—speaks to the profound and enduring nature of scientific inquiry. As we delve deeper into the unknown, each discovery not only answers old questions but also generates new ones, perpetuating a ceaseless journey of exploration that may well define the future trajectory of human civilization.

CHAPTER 24
LANGUAGE AND MATHMATICS

In this chapter, we discuss the intriguing notion that language shapes our knowledge, and delve into the role of mathematics as the universal language of nature, offering insights into the infinite and possibly unknowable horizons of the natural world.

Some argue that language determines the limits of our knowledge. However, rather than restricting what we can know, language primarily serves as a tool for describing and communicating our understanding. Humans have continuously evolved language, inventing new terms and concepts to articulate novel discoveries and ideas. This adaptability underscores the fact that language expands rather than constrains our pursuit of knowledge, particularly in the realm of natural sciences.

The historical roots of using mathematics to decode nature trace back to the ancient Greeks, notably the Pythagoreans. They recognized that musical pitches correspond to mathematical ratios and saw numerical relationships in geometrical figures. From these observations, they hypothesized that such mathematical relationships could be the key to understanding the cosmos itself—a monumental leap in conceptual thinking.

This intuition has yielded more insights than the Pythagoreans could have ever imagined. Centuries later, the profound connection between mathematics and the natural world was eloquently described by physicist Richard Feynman. In his book, *The Character of Physical Law*, Feynman articulated that to appreciate nature, one must understand the mathematical language in which she communicates. This idea reinforces the notion that mathematics does not just describe the universe; it reveals its hidden layers.

The relationship between mathematics and the natural world becomes even more intriguing when considering the work of twentieth-century logician Kurt Gödel. Gödel's incompleteness theorems demonstrated that in any consistent, axiomatically defined mathematical system, there are truths that cannot be proven within the system itself. These truths, however, might be provable by expanding the system's axiomatic basis. This implies that the universe of mathematical truths is potentially infinite, suggesting that our understanding of the natural world could also be without end.

Alonso Church's 'paradox of unknowability' further complicates our quest for knowledge. Church posited that unless one possesses complete knowledge, there will always be truths that remain inherently unknowable. This concept is particularly poignant in the context of the physical universe. Considering that most of the universe is unobservable and possibly infinite, it is likely that vast swathes of it will remain perpetually beyond our comprehension.

THE UNSOLVABLE PROBLEM

Frederic Fitch's 1963 paper, "A Logical Analysis of Some Value Concepts," presents a proof, now known as Theorem 5, which fundamentally challenges the distinctions between different types of ignorance—specifically, contingent ignorance and necessary ignorance. This theorem posits that the existence of any unknown truth implies the existence of truths that are necessarily unknowable. Formally stated, Theorem 5 is expressed as $\exists p(p \wedge \neg Kp) \vdash \exists p(p \wedge \neg \Diamond Kp)$, meaning that if there is a truth that is unknown, then there must be truths that cannot possibly be known.

The paradox, often referred to as the "Knowability Paradox," arises from the contrapositive of Theorem 5, suggesting that if a truth can be known, then it must already be known, essentially collapsing potential knowledge into actual knowledge. This outcome leads to a theoretical extreme where sophisticated anti-realism converges into naive idealism, a shift most philosophers would prefer to avoid as it dismisses the nuanced philosophical positions that recognize unknowable truths while maintaining a critical stance towards anti-realism.

This paradox was first hinted at in a proof sent to Fitch by Alonzo Church in 1945, although Fitch published the formal proof later in response to a specific problem related to his analysis of value. Though the broader philosophical community initially overlooked this discussion, it gained significant attention in the late 1970s and early 1980s, particularly as a critique and potential refutation of verificationism—the idea that all meaningful statements must be empirically verifiable.

Since then, the Knowability Paradox has been a focal point for debates on the limitations of epistemic theories of truth. The paradox argues against the idea that all truths are potentially knowable, suggesting instead that some truths are inherently beyond human understanding. This conclusion challenges verificationism and similar philosophies that claim all truths must, in principle, be accessible to human inquiry.

Philosophical discourse around this topic has explored whether the original proof by Fitch might involve any logical errors or whether the implications of the paradox necessitate a revision of classical logic itself. Some philosophers, like Timothy Williamson, have suggested adopting intuitionistic logic, which allows for a verificationist interpretation of negation and existential quantification and does not assume the law of double negation, thereby avoiding the paradox's conclusion that all truths are known.

Others propose that Fitch's conclusions require a revision of not just logical standards but also a deeper examination of the epistemic assumptions underlying the knowability principle. For instance, the application of paraconsistent logic, where contradictions do not lead to logical explosion, has been considered as a means to manage the paradox's more problematic implications.

Further exploration and debate continue to determine the most philosophically robust and logically consistent response to the Knowability Paradox. Whether through modifying the scope of what is considered knowable, adopting different logical frameworks, or revising the underlying assumptions about knowledge and truth, the discussion remains central to contemporary epistemology. Each proposed solution reflects a deeper philosophical inquiry into the nature of truth, knowledge, and the limits of human understanding, highlighting the ongoing complexity and dynamism of philosophical exploration in addressing foundational questions of epistemology.

As we advance our understanding, the limits of knowledge—both mathematical and physical—appear as a horizon that continuously retreats before us. This metaphorical horizon not only encapsulates the vast, uncharted territories of knowledge but also symbolizes the ongoing, infinite journey of scientific discovery.

Thus, while some may view the boundaries of language and mathematics as constraints, they are more accurately seen as the frameworks through which we expand our understanding of the universe. As we probe deeper into the nature of reality, propelled by the evolving language of mathematics, we continually push the boundaries of what was once thought unknowable. This chapter, therefore, explores how our expanding grasp of mathematical principles continues to shape our understanding of the universe, suggesting that the true limits of what we can know might forever elude us, urging us ever onward in our quest for knowledge.

CHAPTER 25

ASIMOV'S VISION AND THE ULTIMATE QUESTION

This chapter explores the profound idea that the limits of knowledge are reached only when the last question has been asked—and answered. Through the lens of Isaac Asimov's visionary short story, "The Last Question," we ponder whether knowledge can ever be truly complete, and what it would mean to ask and answer the final question of the universe.

Isaac Asimov's seminal 1956 short story "The Last Question" tackles a deceptively straightforward query with profound implications: what will transpire when entropy inevitably extinguishes the final star in the universe? This monumental question is first posed to Multivac, Asimov's fictional ultra-advanced computer system possessing unprecedented processing power and analytical capabilities. Yet even Multivac's response - "There is, as yet, insufficient data for a meaningful answer" - underscores the persistent limitations in humanity's quest for knowledge.

As billions of years pass, Asimov traces Multivac's continual evolution into an immense, galaxy-spanning intelligence. Despite its ever-expanding

THE UNSOLVABLE PROBLEM

powers of computation and assimilation of phenomenal amounts of data, Multivac repeatedly fails to resolve that ultimate question about the cosmos's end state. The computer's persistent answer echoes the enduring struggle to push the boundaries of knowledge: insufficient data exists to reach a definitive conclusion. Asimov provocatively suggests that certain problems may remain unsolvable even given near godlike intellect and eons of accrued information. The story's elegance derives from the deceiving simplicity of its central question, which probes the constraints on comprehension itself.

The narrative progresses through trillions of years, capturing the evolution of life and technology until the universe approaches its quiet end. As the last star dims and the final form of intelligent life—a spectral, ethereal entity—merges with Multivac, the question is asked once more. Still, the answer is the same: insufficient data. However, when all stars have extinguished and the universe succumbs to darkness, Multivac, now alone with all the knowledge of the cosmos, finally uncovers the answer. Yet, with no one left to hear, it chooses to demonstrate rather than state the answer, culminating in the profound declaration: "Let there be light!"

This thought-provoking narrative raises a pivotal question that strikes at the heart of the quest for knowledge: If the accumulation of information and understanding continues to expand until the very last query is definitively resolved, what then constitutes the ultimate question? Is it conceivable that the final mystery we seek to unravel is whether humanity can ever fully comprehend how all the diverse elements of the universe fit together and interconnect in perfect harmony? Could the long-awaited answer to this profound question also finally reveal the underlying reason why everything in existence was created in the first place?

The intriguing proposition that the limits of human knowledge are only reached when everything is completely known and understood invites us to carefully consider whether such a state of absolute understanding and enlightenment is truly achievable—or even ultimately desirable. This idea prompts deep reflection on the fundamental nature of questions and answers: how each discovery often leads organically to new questions arising, suggesting a potentially infinite progression of ongoing inquiry and revelation. As knowledge expands, does comprehension increase correspondingly? Or does the realization of how much remains unknown only expand in tandem, with answers merely uncovering further layers of questions?

Thus, Asimov's story serves not only as a reflection on the limits of human and artificial intelligence but also as a metaphor for the scientific endeavor itself. It encapsulates the essence of scientific inquiry: an eternal cycle of questions and answers that drive the expansion of knowledge.

While the story of Multivac provides a speculative look at the ultimate fate of knowledge, it also emphasizes a critical aspect of human inquiry: as long as there are entities capable of questioning the universe, the journey of knowledge will never truly end. This chapter challenges us to consider the philosophical and practical implications of pursuing the ultimate answers, inviting a deeper contemplation of what it means to know, to ask, and to understand the cosmos.

CHAPTER 26
MIND, INFORMATION, AND OMNISCIENCE

In this chapter, we delve into the philosophical dimensions of knowledge, exploring how the limits of knowledge are intrinsically tied to the capacities of the human mind and the boundaries of information. We will examine the idea that once information is perceived by a conscious mind, it transforms into knowledge—data that can be creatively utilized.

To fully grasp the limits of knowledge, we must first rigorously define what knowledge itself fundamentally entails. Knowledge, in its most basic form, can be conceptualized as quanta of substantive information that have been received and consciously processed by a sentient entity. Without the presence of such a receptive consciousness to actively interpret it, information remains inert and diffuse, simply one small constituent piece of the vast cosmic fabric on par with elementary particles and energy. However, once apprehended and integrated by a sapient mind, information transforms and evolves beyond mere data points; instead, it becomes a dynamic tool for creativity, innovation, and imagination—the very building blocks of knowledge.

The endless quest for knowledge, undertaken by humans and artificial intelligence alike, inevitably arrives at the precarious boundaries imposed by the inherent capabilities of the probing mind itself and the intrinsic limits of the information it seeks to understand. While the exact coordinates of these conceptual limits remain nebulous and challenging to identify with precision, it stands to reason that there exists an upper threshold beyond which the human mind simply cannot venture. This threshold perhaps defines the final frontier—the apex which encapsulates the maximum potential limits of human knowledge. Yet, the abstract domain of information itself appears theoretically infinite, encompassing all things within the farthest reaches of multidimensional space and time. Therefore, if a sufficiently advanced intellect were ever able to fully assimilate, comprehend, and reflect the sum totality of information across all planes of existence, it would, by definition, attain a state of omniscience—absolute and consummate knowledge across all spheres.

The staggering magnitude of omniscience compels us to consider whether any form of mind, either natively biological or artificially devised, could realistically ever evolve to such a supremely exalted state of integral understanding. In speculative fields like theoretical physics or highly advanced computational architectures, some posit that future iterations of artificial superintelligence may perhaps harness the astronomical energy of entire galaxies or even tap directly into the elemental forces structuring the cosmos itself, thereby approaching a level of knowledge on par with the divine—a perspective once solely confined to the realms of science fiction, vividly explored by pioneering authors like Arthur C. Clarke and his visions of technologically sublime civilizations, or Olaf Stapledon with his unbounded cosmic vantage points, but now conceivably approaching the realm of scientific reality. This concept also profoundly echoes religious and philosophical models of a singular omniscient deity—a being often described as fully transcending the known physical universe and operating beyond conventional laws of space and time altogether.

This line of thought ushers us into a deep ontological query: If an unfathomably advanced cosmic intellect or divine being were to understand facets of reality that fundamentally expand beyond our observable universe, would this extracellular awareness still qualify asknowledge, as we narrowly define the concept from our limited human vantage point? This question forces us to inspect, ontologically, the very building blocks of knowledge itself—its structure, origins, and defining characteristics. It also opens lively debate between philosophers, theologians, scientists, and technologists as each perspective contributes its unique insights. The very notion of a deity possessing comprehension of realms inaccessible and inconceivable to us pushes our abstract dialogues into precarious territories where even language itself begins to falter and lose coherence. The semantic tools and conceptual vehicles productive for common human experience become insufficient as we attempt to articulate and frame these radical frontiers of thought.

When discussing an omniscient being, for example, we find that traditional descriptors and linguistic frameworks often cannot fully encapsulate such an entity. Our language strains against its boundaries, suggesting that customary human modes of understanding fail to completely capture the essence of this transcendent abstraction. This very struggle highlights a pivotal philosophical truth: the limits of our language frequently demark the limits of our conceptual world. As Ludwig Wittgenstein observed, the limits of my language mean the limits of my world, implying that anything we cannot articulate in words we must simply pass over in silence.

Therefore, the philosophical pursuit of omniscience not only expands the horizons of how we define knowledge itself but also dramatically impacts our understanding of what forms of consciousness, whether organic or artificial, can potentially attain it. It stimulates ongoing discourse bridging the fields of philosophy, theology, science, and technology as we collectively seek to understand the ultimate thresholds of knowledge. As both technology and our conceptual frameworks evolve, perhaps entirely new languages and schools of thought will emerge that prove better equipped to discuss and contextualize such unfathomably complex ideas.

Understanding the extreme frontiers of knowledge and omniscience remains a dynamically evolving field as technology progresses and philosophical inquiry deepens. It continuously challenges our assumptions about the nature of the universe, the essence of knowledge, and the latent capabilities of consciousness to apprehend and accurately depict the intricate workings of existence. As we progressively unveil and examine these questions, we not only expand our intellectual horizons but also refine our appreciation for the profundity of what it means to genuinely know in its deepest sense. The quest itself is enlightening.

CHAPTER 27
INCOMPREHENSIBILITY OF KNOWLEDGE

In the vast cosmos of human inquiry, we are but intrepid explorers—venturing forth to map the uncharted territories of understanding. Yet even as our expeditions yield breathtaking revelations, we find ourselves confronting impassable frontiers—dividing lines that separate the knowable from the inscrutable unknown. These boundaries manifest in two distinct forms: domains rendered inaccessible by the ravages of time and circumstance, and realms so profound that they defy comprehension by the very architecture of our minds. The former represents knowledge's low-hanging fruit—merely beyond our grasp, not our faculties. The latter, however, presents an existential challenge, questioning the very limits of human cognition itself.

Let us first examine those truths rendered untouchable by cruel happenstance rather than innate complexity. In this murky realm, the mists of time conspire to shroud whole civilizations in inscrutable ambiguity. We gaze back to ancient Rome, where each corporeal detail of daily banality has dissipated like the ashes of a dying fire. What humble repast might Julius Caesar have broken his morning fast upon in the sun-drenched youth of his reign? Alas, that trivial morsel of knowledge lies forever sequestered behind the veil of centuries lost to dust. Curiosities abound across history's sprawling tapestry—tantalizing disconnects where circumstance has callously occluded understanding. We may never unravel the specific designs gracing the walls of Babylon or the peculiar inflections with which Socrates spun his verbal wizardry. Yet these voids ultimately reveal less about the limits of our comprehension than the fragility of record keeping itself.

Mathematics presents another vast frontier where inaccessibility persists, though of a more structured variety. Here, human ingenuity teeters between formulaic illumination and the void of mystery, separated only by the fraying thread of cognition. Take, for instance, the Goldbach Conjecture's eternal dance with uncertainty. First posed in 1742, it offers a simple supposition: that every even number beyond two represents the sum of two prime values. An elegant concept—yet despite millennia of tireless human exertion, no mind has produced a conclusive proof. Not for lack of collective brilliance, but rather due to methodological limitations. Certain mathematical truths may persist in the dark beyond our ability to shed computative light, shrouded in complexity but not unfathomability.

As tantalizing as this form of inaccessibility may be, there exists a far more profound and disquieting breed of mystery. These are the boundaries not of methodology but of innate human comprehension itself. The questions that lurk at perception's event horizon, daring us to stare into the abyss of the incomprehensible.

In the dim recesses of the human mind's own inner cosmos, an impenetrable puzzle looms—the enigma of consciousness itself. We have unraveled so many secrets of the cerebral expanse through neuroscience's intrepid forays—how networks of electrochemical neurons spark perception, encoding experiences as memories. And yet, the core essence of conscious awareness defies every attempt at demystification. What IS this kaleidoscope of subjective sensations we each experience? How does the cacophony of neurotransmitters coalesce into the felt firmness of a unified sense of self? For all our scientific progress illuminating consciousness's biological architecture, its fundamental nature persists in obscurity.

The notion of cognitive closure offers a harrowing explanation—proposing the human mind may be inherently deficient in capacities required to answer certain cosmic riddles. Like the mythological Minotaur futilely raging against the labyrinth walls constraining its own sentience, we face stark boundaries beyond which our reasoning tools cease to function. Consciousness could represent precisely that—a phenomenon so alien to our natural experiences that its true essence will eternally elude our conceptual grasp. We may chart its biological peripheries but never penetrate its deepest existential core. This brutal hypothesis leaves us adrift, our journey of self-discovery cut shamefully short at the intersection of logic and mind.

Uncomfortable existential dilemmas linger at this murky event horizon too. The interminable tangle of free will and determinism—a question humanity has wrestled with since our dawning sentience. If our choices stem from electrified networks of chemically-triggered neurons, are our actions anything more than domino waves set inevitably in motion by prior causes? Or is there some quintessential spark of autonomous agency we simply cannot perceive from our limited vantage point?

More nettlesome still is the question from which all others seem to stem— the primordial void from which existence itself bubbled forth: Why is there something rather than nothing? This is the abyss into which all other interrogatives inevitably collapsed, their mass crushed under the gravitational immensity of the ultimate cosmic mystery. On this, science offers no insights, no conceptual frameworks. For our entire enterprise of understanding takes as its axiomatic starting point that existence simply IS. All our brilliant theories and cosmic visions draw their first breath from that primordial given.

CHAPTER 28

THE CONSTRAINTS ON KNOWLEDGE

This chapter delves deeply into the various factors that limit our capacity for knowledge. These constraints arise from the inherent boundaries of our brains, senses, language, personal experiences, imagination, and the technologies we employ to understand the world. Collectively, these limitations define the scope and depth of human understanding, shaping how we perceive and interact with our surroundings.

Our brains have a finite ability to process information and detect patterns. This capacity profoundly influences skills like mathematical reasoning, critical analysis, and problem solving. The speed at which we can absorb new information and spot connections directly impacts how well we grasp intricate concepts. Furthermore, the sophistication of our thought and communication relies heavily on our mental faculties. As George Orwell highlighted with Newspeak in his classic dystopian novel 1984, restricting language can dramatically limit the ideas we are able to formulate and articulate. Thus, the cognitive abilities encoded in our brains constitute a fundamental barrier to knowledge.

Additionally, our innate sensory apparatus delineates natural boundaries on our perception of the external world. While tools like microscopes, telescopes and spectrometers have greatly augmented our senses, we still only ever achieve an incomplete representation of any object we examine. As the philosopher Immanuel Kant discussed, our perception of things is filtered through the lens of our unique experiences and colored by the intrinsic constraints of our sensory organs. Thus, our faculties of perception pose additional obstacles to attaining comprehensive knowledge.

Imagination and creativity are key for innovation, yet our ability to envision novel concepts depends directly on our existing knowledge and experiences. In a sense, innovation involves recombining familiar ideas into new configurations and applications. For instance, while ancient Romans were certainly familiar with the process of heating bread, their ignorance of electricity made conceiving of a toaster impossible. This demonstrates how our current understanding and historical situation define our capacity to imagine future advances.

Finally, the tools and technologies used to interrogate nature themselves have inescapable limitations that bound what we can potentially observe and quantify. Though scientific instruments have vastly expanded the phenomena we can study, from distant galaxies to quantum particles, they are inevitably constrained by factors like measurement accuracy, operating ranges, precision levels, and many other variables. Every technique and apparatus contains intrinsic constraints dictated by its constituent materials, operational principles, calibration needs, and the contexts where it functions optimally.

By scrutinizing the various factors that restrict our intelligence - whether cognitive, perceptual, technological or historical - we gain insight into why certain knowledge remains elusive. But this analysis also illuminates potential routes to overcome our limitations through cognitive enhancement, technological progress and interdisciplinary collaboration. As we push back the boundaries of what our brains and instruments can handle, we continuously redefine the outer limits of human understanding. Thus, the very factors that constrain our grasp of the world also propel us to surpass these barriers and uncover new realms of knowledge. Our voyage toward greater comprehension is directed both by the restrictions we seek to transcend and the tantalizing possibilities that lie just beyond our present reach.

CHAPTER 29
THE INFINITE POSSIBILITIES OF KNOWLEDGE

In this exploration of the limits of knowledge, we confront both the physical constraints of data storage and the more abstract, philosophical boundaries that define what can be known. While the capacity to record and store knowledge is undeniably limited by available resources—whether they be digital storage media or the human brain itself—these resources are finite and thus set a ceiling on how much information can be preserved and accessed over time.

However, the philosophical limits of knowledge present a more complex and intriguing challenge. Ludwig Wittgenstein's famous proposition, "Whereof one cannot speak, thereof one must be silent," suggests that if we lack the language or concepts to describe something, we cannot meaningfully discuss it. This might initially seem to mark a clear boundary of knowledge. Yet history shows that humanity does not simply accept these limitations; instead, it continually develops new terminologies and tools to expand understanding. Rather than being silenced by the unknown, we often devise new ways to articulate and explore it.

THE UNSOLVABLE PROBLEM

The progression of human cognitive tools—from the inception of language to the creation of writing, from the development of mathematics to the invention of various technologies—has significantly extended our cognitive reach. These tools have not only enhanced our ability to think and communicate but have also opened new vistas of comprehension that our ancestors could scarcely have imagined. This demonstrates that our conceptual and communicative limitations are not fixed but are instead dynamic, expanding as we evolve culturally and technologically.

Consider the example set forth by philosopher Thomas Nagel in his essay "What Is It Like to Be a Bat?" Nagel posits that some subjective experiences, such as seeing, might be inherently impossible to convey to someone who has never had that sensation—like explaining color to a person blind from birth. However, emerging technologies in direct brain stimulation are beginning to challenge even this seemingly insurmountable barrier, potentially enabling us to share experiences directly through technological means, rather than through descriptive language alone.

The ongoing innovation in cognitive tools and technologies suggests that many of the limits we face today may be surmountable tomorrow. If there are ultimate boundaries to what can be known, the only way to discover these limits is by relentlessly pushing into the unknown, continually expanding the frontier of what is knowable. Each new discovery and technological advancement has the potential to redefine these boundaries, suggesting that the realm of the unknowable might shrink as our capabilities grow.

While we must acknowledge the practical constraints on data storage and the historical limits on our expressive capabilities, the pattern of human development shows a consistent trend toward overcoming such barriers. The pursuit of knowledge is an evolving journey, not defined by what is currently unknown, but propelled forward by an enduring quest to understand more deeply and completely. The question of whether there are absolute limits to knowledge remains open, but the human spirit of inquiry ensures that we will continue to test those boundaries, wherever they may lie.

CHAPTER 30
EVOLUTION OF KNOWLEDGE EXPANSION

In the ever-evolving landscape of academia and intellectual pursuit, the first award of a PhD in Art Education in the UK marked a significant milestone. This event not only heralded the birth of a new academic discipline but also emphasized the transformative power of synthesizing different fields of study. This fusion of disciplines underscored a broader trend in knowledge expansion—a trend well articulated by Melvin Bragg, presenter of BBC Radio 4's *In Our Time*, who described our era as the "greatest age of expanding knowledge, a tumult of erupting knowledge." Such an expansion supports the idea that the boundaries of what we can learn and understand are continually pushed forward by our intellectual endeavors.

The creation of new academic fields like Art Education demonstrates that knowledge is not static; it grows both within distinct disciplines and at the intersections of multiple fields. The synergistic combination of diverse academic realms often leads to the emergence of new areas of study, each representing a novel perspective that could not have been fully realized through the isolated advancement of its component subjects. This phenomenon is a testament to the dynamic nature of human inquiry, which constantly seeks to extend the scope and depth of understanding.

Moreover, the notion that we might someday reach the limits of what can be known seems increasingly unlikely as we continue to develop technologies that extend our natural faculties. Immanuel Kant, the renowned philosopher, famously posited that humans are bound by the 'irremovable spectacles' of space and time, which shape all our perceptions. According to Kant, the noumenal world—the world as it exists independently of human perception—is fundamentally inaccessible to us. However, the rapid advancement of technology challenges this Kantian view by enhancing our sensory capacities and augmenting our cognitive faculties.

Today, technological innovations in fields such as neuroimaging, artificial intelligence, and quantum computing are revolutionizing how we access, process, and understand information. These technologies are not merely tools for extending our existing senses; they create new avenues for experiencing and interacting with the world. For instance, scanning technologies can reveal aspects of physical and biological environments that are invisible to the naked eye, and computational models can simulate complex phenomena that our unaided minds would struggle to grasp.

The potential for technology to break down the traditional barriers of human understanding suggests that the expansion of knowledge may indeed be limitless. With each technological advance, we are able to perceive the world with greater clarity and at resolutions previously unimaginable. Moreover, as we continue to refine these tools, we may even begin to transcend the traditional human categories of understanding, venturing into realms of knowledge that were once thought to be permanently beyond our grasp.

While we consider the future of knowledge, it becomes apparent that the limits of what we can know are continually being redefined by our technological progress and intellectual curiosity. This boundless horizon of understanding invites us to consider not just what we can currently comprehend, but also the vast potential of what might still lie within the reach of future generations. Thus, the journey of expanding knowledge is not one that approaches a finite endpoint, but rather one that continually opens new doors, posing ever more complex questions that challenge us to think deeper, explore further, and understand more profoundly.

CHAPTER 31
LIMITS OF HUMAN UNDERSTANDING

"Ne plus ultra," Latin for "nothing further beyond," was historically inscribed on the Pillars of Hercules, symbolizing the boundaries of the known world and warning navigators not to sail beyond. Immanuel Kant, in his seminal work *The Critique of Pure Reason* (1781), draws a parallel between these ancient markers and the boundaries of human knowledge. He argues that just as these pillars warned sailors, so too must we recognize the natural limits that confine the voyage of our reason.

Prior to Kant, the prevailing assumption was that human knowledge needed to conform to the objects of sensory experience—that our minds were essentially passive recipients of sensory data. Kant revolutionized this view, positing instead that the objects of sensory experience conform to the cognitive faculties of the mind. According to Kant, the world as it is given to us is shaped by the structure and activity of our minds. This leads to his assertion that fundamental aspects of our experience, such as time and space, are not external realities but rather innate forms of human perception. Our minds come pre-equipped with categories of understanding that organize and synthesize sensory data into the coherent experience of a world structured by time and space.

The implication of Kant's theory is profound: we cannot perceive anything outside of these a priori forms. Anything that exists independently of time or space, or which does not conform to our innate categories of understanding, is inherently unknowable to us. Thus, we do not—and cannot—know the noumenal world, or things as they truly are in themselves. Instead, we only know the phenomenal world, or things as they appear to us through the lens of our perceptual and cognitive frameworks.

Given these inherent limitations, Kant warns against the hubris of attempting to extend the reach of human reason beyond the "continuous coastline of experience." He argues that it is futile to speculate on matters such as the intrinsic nature of the universe, the existence of God, the soul, free will, or immortality using the tools of pure reason. Such ventures, he suggests, will lead us astray into realms of speculation where no secure knowledge is possible—akin to sailors venturing beyond the Pillars of Hercules into uncharted waters.

Kant's philosophical caution serves as a critical reminder of the limits of human inquiry. By defining the boundaries of what can be known, he does not diminish the pursuit of knowledge but rather clarifies its scope and nature. This philosophical demarcation helps us understand that while we can aspire to deepen our knowledge within the phenomenal world—the world as shaped by human cognition—we must recognize that some aspects of reality remain beyond the reach of human understanding.

In this chapter, we reflect on the implications of Kant's philosophy for contemporary knowledge pursuits. How do we balance the ambitious drive for knowledge with the humble recognition of our cognitive limits? What does it mean for scientific inquiry and philosophical speculation when we accept that certain questions may lie forever beyond our grasp? These are not merely academic questions but are central to how we understand our place in the cosmos and the nature of reality itself. As we continue to push the boundaries of knowledge, Kant's philosophical insights remind us to navigate these waters with caution, respecting the natural limits that define the human condition.

CHAPTER 32
TYPES, TRUTHS, AND THEORETICAL LIMITS

In this chapter, we delve into the multifaceted nature of knowledge, exploring its different forms and the philosophical challenges of defining what it means to truly "know" something. This exploration is not merely an academic exercise but a journey through the deep and sometimes contentious debates within philosophy about knowledge itself. By dissecting various classifications of knowledge, analyzing the traditional philosophical definition of justified true belief (JTB), and considering Karl Popper's influential theories on the limits and nature of scientific knowledge, we gain a comprehensive view of how knowledge is structured and understood across different fields and epochs.

Knowledge can be categorized into several types, each playing a unique role in how we understand and interact with the world. Declarative knowledge, or "knowing that," involves facts and information, such as knowing that Washington, D.C. is the capital of the United States. Procedural knowledge, or "knowing how," refers to the skills and processes through which tasks are performed, such as knowing how to ride a bicycle. Personal knowledge encompasses intimate experiences and emotions, reflecting a subjective understanding of one's own internal states—an example of this could be the profound and unique grief one feels upon losing a loved one, which cannot be fully understood by others who haven't experienced a similar loss. Shared knowledge represents ideas and beliefs that are widely accepted within communities and cultures, forming the basis of collective understanding and social norms.

Sir Karl Popper further elaborated on these distinctions with his theory of "three worlds." In Popper's framework, World 1 is the physical universe, including all physical objects and states. World 2 consists of all subjective (personal) knowledge, encompassing mental states and individual consciousness. World 3 contains knowledge existing independently of individual minds—this includes stories, theories, mathematical constructs, scientific concepts, cultural beliefs, and intellectual creations. Popper's delineation of these worlds helps clarify the interplay between subjective experiences and the objective, communal repositories of human thought and understanding. This framework is essential for discussing knowledge, as it allows us to categorize and examine the dynamics between personal insights and the collective intellectual landscape.

A widely accepted philosophical definition of knowledge is Socrates' concept of Justified True Belief (JTB). According to this framework, for an individual to know a proposition p, three conditions must be met: the individual must believe that p is true; p must indeed be true; and there must be sufficient justification (through evidence, good reasons, or sound argument) for believing p to be true. However, the JTB theory faces significant challenges, particularly illustrated by Edmund Gettier's cases, which demonstrate that a person can have justified beliefs that are incidentally true but not due to the reasons they believe. For example, a person might correctly believe it is 2 pm based on a stopped clock that happens to show the correct time purely by chance. These scenarios reveal that even well-supported beliefs might not constitute true knowledge if the justification is flawed or coincidental.

Karl Popper contributed profoundly to our understanding of the empirical limits of knowledge through his concept of falsification. Popper argued that scientific knowledge is provisional: a theory remains scientific only if it is falsifiable—that is, it can be proven false. For instance, the statement "all swans are white" can be falsified by the observation of a single black swan. According to Popper, knowledge is inherently incomplete, as our understanding is always subject to revision based on new evidence. This perspective aligns with Albert Einstein's reflection that with every increase in knowledge, our awareness of ignorance also grows.

Thus, the pursuit of knowledge is a dynamic and ongoing process, characterized by an ever-expanding frontier of questions and uncertainties. As we continue to explore the vast landscape of knowledge, from the deeply personal to the universally empirical, we are continually reminded of the provisional nature of our understanding. Each piece of knowledge we acquire opens new avenues of inquiry, suggesting that the quest for understanding is, indeed, limitless. This chapter invites readers to appreciate the complexity of knowledge, recognizing both its power and its limitations, as we strive to navigate and expand the boundaries of human understanding.

CHAPTER 33
CONTROVERSIES OF INBORN UNDERSTANDING

In the exploration of human cognition and the origins of knowledge, one of the most intriguing and contentious topics is the concept of innate knowledge—ideas and abilities with which we are purportedly born. This chapter delves into the psychological and philosophical dimensions of this debate, examining why the acceptance of innate knowledge poses such a challenge, both intellectually and culturally.

Northeastern psychology professor Iris Berent has dedicated significant research to understanding how humans acquire complex skills such as language. Echoing the theories of renowned linguists like Noam Chomsky, Berent and her colleagues suggest that the human potential for language is an innate capability. This theory is supported by observations of children who can formulate entirely new sentences—ones they have never heard before—indicating an intrinsic linguistic ability.

Despite the empirical evidence supporting the notion of innate language faculties, Berent discovered through her research that many people—

ranging from laypersons to fellow scientists—are resistant to the idea that such knowledge can be inborn. This resistance is so pervasive that it prompted Berent to investigate its origins. Her findings suggest that humans possess an "innate antinativist" bias—an ingrained reluctance to accept that we are born with certain knowledge.

Yet even as we probe the farthest horizons of human knowledge, seeking to illuminate the unsolvable mysteries that circle comprehension's outermost bounds, another fundamental enigma lurks closer at hand – an innate blindness that shrouds our understanding of cognition itself. For despite compelling scientific revelations, a deep-rooted bias persists, an intuitive resistance to the notion that knowledge could ever be truly inborn.

This enduring reluctance reveals an unsolvable problem woven into the very fabric of our thinking – the tendency to intimately associate inheritance with tangible physical attributes alone. It is a conceptual handicap stemming from our primitive grasp of biological reproduction, where corporeal traits clearly transmit across generations. But could something as intangible as knowledge – the subtle stuff of consciousness itself – also dwell innately within us, imprinted into the nervous system's structure? To many, this prospect defies intuition, clashing with our most basic assumptions about learning and experience.

After all, it seems self-evident that knowledge is wholly derived through environmental exposure – an accumulated mass of lessons gleaned from sensory engagement with the outside world. How could the nebulous content of understanding pre-exist the mind's own developmental journey? Would this not render experience fundamentally redundant? This line of scepticism exposes the profound bias at the heart of our folk psychology of learning – the belief that the blank slate of consciousness is gradually inscribed through external stimulation alone.

Yet empirically, the evidence for innate cognition continues to mount, most compellingly within the domain of language acquisition. Children routinely exhibit remarkable linguistic faculties, rapidly acquiring grammatical mastery at a pace that appears to outstrip environmental conditioning. Such observations led Noam Chomsky to formulate his groundbreaking theory of universal grammar – the notion that human brains arrive innately equipped with foundational parameters for constructing syntax, independent of any tutelage.

This research demands a seismic revision of how we conceive of cognition's origins, forcing us to relinquish the seductive metaphor of the mind as a tabula rasa. Instead, we must envision the nervous system's impossibly intricate neural architecture as a product of deep evolutionary genesis – a phylogenetic feat embedding innate literacies within the very genetic source code of Homo sapiens.

Here then, cloaked within our own psychology, lies an unsolvable problem equal in profundity to the cosmic mysteries that orbit comprehension's most distant frontiers. For in recoiling from innate knowledge, we exhibit the pernicious constraints of cognitive entrenchment – whereby our naive folk assumptions actively inhibit deeper insight. It is a self-propagating paradox in which ignorance itself occludes understanding, as the blind spots embedded within our thinking obstruct further enlightenment.

To progress, we must overcome this innate resistance by fully embracing the prospect of pre-installed comprehension. For this unsolvable problem is no mere philosophical distraction, but a direct impediment to elucidating the true wellspring of human intelligence. We must remain radically open to dismantling outdated frameworks that reduce learning to passive environmental inscription. While the boundless enigmas of the cosmos may eternally confound, the problem of innate knowledge holds the key to unlocking cognition from its own innate confinement.

THE UNSOLVABLE PROBLEM

As we push comprehension's horizons, both outward and inward, we must recognize the shackles imposed by folk assumptions that reduce knowledge to sensory artifacts alone. For the unsolvable mysteries of mind stretch endlessly in two directions – challenging us to transcend subjective blindness at each turn. Only by confronting the unsolvable problem of innate ignorance can we hope to reveal the hidden substrates from which human intellect blossoms. With each inborn aptitude discovered, from linguistic fluency to mathematical reasoning, another veil is lifted, exposing the true foundations underlying cognition's most splendid edifice.

CHAPTER 34
ENTSCHEIDUNGSPROBLEM

The Entscheidungsproblem, or "decision problem," stands as a cornerstone of theoretical computer science and mathematical logic. Initially posed by German mathematician David Hilbert in the early 20th century, the Entscheidungsproblem was a central part of Hilbert's ambitious program to formalize all of mathematics. Hilbert envisioned a systematic approach where a set of axioms could determine the truth or falsehood of any mathematical proposition. Addressing this problem was essential for realizing Hilbert's vision of a completely mechanized and formalized mathematics where assertions could universally be proven true or false.

Hilbert's challenge directly asked whether there exists a universal algorithmic method capable of solving any mathematical question definitively by answering "true" or "false." The pursuit of such a method held the promise of transforming mathematics into a discipline where all statements could be resolved through clear, mechanical procedures, eliminating the need for intuition or ambiguity in mathematical thought.

However, this vision was dramatically reshaped by groundbreaking work in the 1930s, led by mathematicians and logicians like Kurt Gödel, Alonzo

Church, and Alan Turing, each contributing to the problem's ultimate resolution.

Kurt Gödel's Incompleteness Theorems, presented in 1931, were the first to challenge Hilbert's program fundamentally. Gödel demonstrated that any sufficiently powerful formal system capable of arithmetic would inevitably contain true statements that it could not prove. This introduced the concept of "incompleteness," which implies that the axiomatic method as envisioned by Hilbert had intrinsic limitations. Gödel's results suggested that no system of axioms could ever be both complete (capable of proving all truths about arithmetic) and consistent (never proving a false statement).

The final blow to the Entscheidungsproblem came from Alan Turing in 1936 with his introduction of the Turing machine, a theoretical construct that became the foundation for modern computer science. Turing used this model to prove that there is no general algorithmic way to solve the Halting Problem (determining whether any arbitrary computer program will eventually stop or continue to run indefinitely). This result implied that the Entscheidungsproblem was unsolvable; there could be no universal computational method to determine the truth value of every mathematical proposition.

This discovery had profound implications, defining the limits of what could be determined through computation and establishing the field of computability theory. It emphasized that some problems are fundamentally "undecidable," meaning they do not admit a straightforward computational solution. This recognition reshaped the landscape of theoretical computer science by highlighting the inherent limitations of algorithms.

Moreover, the resolution of the Entscheidungsproblem led to the development of complexity theory, which classifies problems based on the computational resources needed to solve them. This area of study has identified various classes of problems, such as P, NP, and PSPACE, based on their computational tractability, further refining our understanding of the computational universe.

In conclusion, the Entscheidungsproblem not only catalyzed significant advancements in mathematics and computer science but also deepened our philosophical understanding of the limits of formal systems. By demonstrating that not all mathematical problems are decidable, the resolution of the Entscheidungsproblem invites ongoing reflection on the nature of problem-solving and the boundaries of algorithmic logic. This chapter not only details a pivotal episode in the history of mathematics but also encourages a broader contemplation of how we define and tackle problems in an increasingly algorithm-driven world.

CHAPTER 35
MILLERS MAGICAL NUMBER

Few works in psychology have attained the legendary status of George Miller's 1956 paper, "The Magical Number Seven, Plus or Minus Two." This seminal piece captured the field's imagination by proposing finite limits on our ability to process information. Yet this widely celebrated article also had an unintended consequence - it paradoxically inhibited research on working memory capacity for over four decades.

Miller's lighthearted framing, portraying himself as "persecuted by an integer," may have inadvertently discouraged scientific scrutiny of his core observations. His quip that any commonality between the capacity limits he described was likely a mere "coincidence" created a subtle deterrent against investigating their potentially deeper connections.

In retrospect, Miller's humorous tone seems to have engendered an unspoken taboo. Probing too earnestly into the precise underpinnings of these processing constraints risked subjecting oneself to ridicule - a fate the pioneering Miller surely never intended. An invisible stigma thus took hold, stifling the field's appetite to methodically unpack the true nature and extent of our mental capacity limits.

It was not until the early 2000s that this implicit avoidance finally dissolved and capacity limits resurfaced as a focal point of inquiry. Propelled by technological advances allowing precise measurement of visual working memory, the field regained its intellectual courage to confront Miller's observations head-on.

Emboldened by neuroimaging techniques and rigorous computational models, researchers could finally put Miller's "magical" findings under the harsh light of empirical scrutiny. No longer confined by the haunting specter of oversimplification, they could pursue nuanced investigations into the Complex symphony of factors constraining our mental bandwidth.

This overdue renaissance revealed Miller's proposals to be rooted in genuine phenomena demanding deeper explication, not merely thought-provoking paradoxes. It sparked vital new lines of research disentangling the roles of time, interference, attention, and sheer information load in bounding cognition.

As the old reservations faded, Miller's magical number gradually emerged as neither whimsy nor inevitability - but a profound clue to the brain's exquisitely balanced information channels. Suddenly, unraveling its truths promised grand insights into the neurological essence of human consciousness itself.

In many ways, the saga of the magical number encapsulates both the tantalizing promise and sobering limitations defining the very quest for knowledge. An idea once sparking amusement and dismissal ultimately revealed itself as a gateway to illuminating the deepest workings of the human mind.

THE UNSOLVABLE PROBLEM

Miller never could have predicted his "persecution" metaphor would unwittingly incept decades of scholarly avoidance behavior. Yet this strange trajectory reminds us that the road to understanding is often winding and paradoxical. The most penetrating truths are frequently obscured by seemingly whimsical exteriors demanding we perceive beyond the superficial.

Ultimately, the greatest impediments to comprehending the unsolvable mysteries of cognition may reside within our own mental blinders - those innate propensities to shy away from daunting complexities through self-handicapping assumptions or facile humor. Only by cultivating a candid openness to life's profound puzzles, embracing their full dimensionality, can we hope to extract insight from the inscrutable.

For just as Miller's magical number itself concealed revelations awaiting rigorous decoding, so too may the path to cognitive enlightenment lie obscured behind the veil of our own psychological defensiveness. The human mind's grandest truths often slumber behind the mask of the deceptively simplistic - daring us to transcend our inevitable first impressions to gain their deepest secrets.

CHAPTER 36
THE SHIP OF THESEUS

In the realm of unsolvable problems, the Ship of Theseus stands as a timeless conundrum that challenges our understanding of identity, continuity, and the nature of objects. This thought experiment, which has its roots in ancient Greek philosophy, raises profound questions about the persistence of an object's essence in the face of change and transformation.

The story of the Ship of Theseus is a familiar one. The Athenians, seeking to preserve the trireme used by their legendary founder and hero-king Theseus, embark on a project of perpetual maintenance. As the ship's components deteriorate over time, they are replaced one by one, until eventually, every original part has been substituted with a new one. This gradual process of replacement gives rise to a perplexing question: At what point does the ship cease to be the original Ship of Theseus and become a fundamentally different vessel?

The paradox deepens with a further twist: What if the discarded original parts are reassembled to create a second ship? Which of the two vessels can then lay claim to being the true Ship of Theseus? This extension of the problem highlights the inherent difficulty in defining the essential nature of an object and the criteria by which we establish its identity.

THE UNSOLVABLE PROBLEM

Philosophers have grappled with the Ship of Theseus paradox for centuries, proposing various solutions and frameworks for understanding the problem. One influential perspective, advanced by philosopher David Lewis, suggests that different parts of objects exist at different times. According to this view, the ship as a whole occupies a certain space and has a specific age, while its individual components, such as the mast or hull, may be younger and occupy only a portion of that space for a limited duration. By conceiving of objects as existing in both space and time, Lewis attempts to reconcile the apparent paradox of an object being in two places at once or two objects overlapping in a single location.

Another common approach, as noted by philosopher Ryan Wasserman, is to distinguish between the ship as an object and the material from which it is composed. This perspective holds that the ship and its constituent parts are distinct entities, even if they occupy the same space at the same time. While this view directly addresses the problem of equating the ship with its components, it requires accepting the seemingly counterintuitive notion of two different objects coexisting in a single location.

Renowned linguist and cognitive scientist Noam Chomsky offers a different take on the Ship of Theseus paradox, arguing that the problem arises from the assumption that what holds true in our minds must also be true in the external world – a position known as externalism. Chomsky suggests that the puzzle speaks more to the workings of our cognitive processes than it does to the actual nature of the ship's identity. While this perspective has gained traction in certain cognitive science circles, it ultimately sidesteps the core philosophical question posed by the paradox.

The Ship of Theseus problem has far-reaching implications that extend beyond the realm of ancient Greek philosophy. In the field of artificial intelligence and machine learning, for example, questions of identity and continuity arise when considering the iterative process of training and updating AI models. As these models are continually refined and their parameters adjusted, at what point do they become fundamentally different entities from their initial configurations? Similarly, in the domain of digital preservation and archiving, the challenge of maintaining the integrity and authenticity of digital objects in the face of technological change and format obsolescence echoes the Ship of Theseus paradox.

Moreover, the problem resonates with contemporary debates surrounding personal identity, the nature of the self, and the persistence of individual essence in the face of physical and psychological change. Just as the Ship of Theseus raises questions about the continuity of an object's identity, we might ask: What constitutes the essential core of a person, and how do we reconcile the notion of a stable self with the constant flux of our bodies, memories, and experiences?

As we reflect on the Ship of Theseus and its place within the constellation of unsolvable problems, we are reminded of the enduring power of philosophical thought experiments to challenge our intuitions and probe the boundaries of our understanding. The paradox invites us to question our assumptions about the nature of reality, the relationship between form and essence, and the limits of language and conceptualization in capturing the complexities of the world.

While the Ship of Theseus may resist a definitive resolution, engaging with the problem enriches our understanding of the fundamental questions that define the human condition. It encourages us to embrace the ambiguity and uncertainty that often characterize our grappling with deep philosophical puzzles, and to find value in the very process of exploration and contemplation.

In the end, the Ship of Theseus stands as a testament to the enduring mystery and complexity of the world, and to the power of the human intellect to confront the most challenging and perplexing aspects of existence. As we navigate the labyrinth of unsolvable problems, the paradox of identity serves as a reminder of the importance of humility, curiosity, and a willingness to engage with the unknown and the unknowable.

CHAPTER 37
CHALLENGES OF ACHIEVING AGI

As we explore the frontiers of artificial intelligence and the quest for Artificial General Intelligence (AGI), it is crucial to consider the role of human knowledge in shaping the development of these advanced systems. While human knowledge serves as a foundation and a guide in the pursuit of AGI, it also carries inherent limitations and gaps that may hinder the realization of truly autonomous and intelligent machines.

At the heart of this challenge lies the recognition that human knowledge is inherently incomplete, fragmented, and subject to various biases and inconsistencies. Despite the vast accumulation of information and expertise across disciplines, there remain numerous domains in which our understanding is limited or even fundamentally flawed. From the mysteries of consciousness and the workings of the human brain to the intricacies of social dynamics and the complexities of the natural world, we are confronted with a myriad of questions and phenomena that defy easy explanation or resolution.

THE UNSOLVABLE PROBLEM

These gaps and limitations in human knowledge pose significant obstacles to the development of AGI systems that can truly rival or surpass human intelligence. If we rely solely on the knowledge and cognitive frameworks that we ourselves possess, we risk constraining the potential of these systems and limiting their ability to generate novel insights, solve complex problems, and adapt to unforeseen challenges.

One of the primary concerns in using human knowledge as the basis for AGI is the propagation of biases and misconceptions. Human understanding is shaped by a complex interplay of cultural, historical, and psychological factors that can lead to erroneous assumptions, prejudices, and blind spots. If these biases are inadvertently encoded into AGI systems, they may perpetuate and amplify the very limitations and flaws that we seek to overcome.

Moreover, the structure and organization of human knowledge itself may pose challenges for the development of AGI. Human understanding is often fragmented and compartmentalized, with deep expertise in specific domains coexisting with significant gaps and inconsistencies across different fields. The lack of a coherent and integrated framework for representing and reasoning about knowledge can hinder the ability of AGI systems to draw meaningful connections, generate novel insights, and engage in the kind of fluid, cross-disciplinary thinking that characterizes human intelligence.

Another fundamental limitation of human knowledge is its grounding in the specific sensory, perceptual, and cognitive capacities of the human mind. Our understanding of the world is mediated by the particular ways in which we process and interpret information, and these mechanisms may not always be optimal or universally applicable. AGI systems that are built upon human knowledge may inherit these constraints and biases, limiting their ability to perceive, reason about, and interact with the world in ways that transcend human limitations.

Furthermore, the pursuit of AGI based on human knowledge raises profound questions about the nature of intelligence itself. Is human intelligence the only or the best model for artificial intelligence? Are there forms of intelligence that are fundamentally different from or even superior to human cognition? By focusing exclusively on replicating or surpassing human knowledge and abilities, we may overlook the potential for AGI systems to develop novel and unconventional forms of intelligence that are adapted to their unique computational substrates and environments.

To overcome these challenges and limitations, researchers and developers in the field of AGI must adopt a multifaceted and interdisciplinary approach. This involves not only drawing upon the wealth of human knowledge across various domains but also actively seeking to identify and address the gaps, biases, and inconsistencies within that knowledge. It requires the development of new frameworks and methodologies for representing, integrating, and reasoning about knowledge in ways that transcend the limitations of human cognition.

Moreover, the pursuit of AGI demands a willingness to explore alternative models and paradigms of intelligence that may depart from human-centric assumptions and constraints. This may involve drawing inspiration from the cognitive processes of other species, exploring the possibilities of non-biological substrates for intelligence, or developing entirely novel architectures and algorithms that are optimized for the unique challenges and opportunities of artificial cognition.

Ultimately, the limitations of human knowledge serve as a reminder of the immense challenges and complexities involved in the quest for AGI. While human understanding provides a valuable starting point and a rich source of inspiration, it is essential to recognize and actively address the gaps, biases, and constraints that may hinder the realization of truly autonomous and intelligent machines.

CHAPTER 38
THE BOUNDARIES OF HUMAN COGNITION

Delving deeper into the nature of human knowledge and its role in shaping our understanding of the world, we are confronted with a fundamental and inescapable reality: our knowledge is ultimately grounded in and constrained by the specific sensory, perceptual, and cognitive capacities of the human mind. These capacities, while remarkable in their own right, also carry inherent limitations that shape and restrict the scope of what we can know and understand.

At the most basic level, human knowledge is acquired through the filter of our sensory experiences. Our eyes, ears, nose, tongue, and skin provide the raw data that forms the foundation of our mental representations and conceptual frameworks. However, these sensory channels are not perfect or exhaustive. They are tuned to specific ranges of stimuli and are subject to various physiological and psychological limitations.

Consider, for example, the human visual system. While our eyes are capable of detecting a wide range of colors and patterns, they are sensitive to only a narrow band of the electromagnetic spectrum. We cannot perceive ultraviolet or infrared light, nor can we see the intricate details of microscopic structures or the vast expanses of the cosmos without the aid of technological enhancements. Moreover, our visual perception is subject to a host of illusions and biases, such as the well-known Müller-Lyer illusion, in which the perceived length of lines is distorted by the presence of arrowheads or tail fins.

Similarly, our auditory system is attuned to a specific range of frequencies and is subject to various perceptual distortions and biases. The McGurk effect, for instance, demonstrates how our perception of speech sounds can be influenced by visual cues, leading to misinterpretations and false impressions. Our sense of taste and smell, while powerful in their ability to evoke memories and emotions, are also limited in their range and sensitivity, and can be easily fooled or overwhelmed by certain stimuli.

These sensory limitations have profound implications for the nature and scope of human knowledge. They remind us that our understanding of the world is not direct or unmediated, but is instead filtered through the particular capacities and constraints of our sensory apparatus. What we perceive and experience is not the world as it is in itself, but rather a specific subset of reality that is accessible to us through the narrow channels of our senses.

Beyond the realm of sensation, human knowledge is also shaped by the cognitive and perceptual processes that operate on the raw data of our experiences. Our minds are not passive receptacles of information, but active and dynamic systems that interpret, organize, and transform the input they receive. These processes, while essential for making sense of the world and navigating its complexities, also introduce their own set of limitations and biases.

One of the most prominent examples of cognitive limitation is the phenomenon of selective attention. Our minds are constantly bombarded with a vast array of sensory stimuli, far more than we can consciously process or attend to at any given moment. To cope with this informational overload, our brains have evolved mechanisms of attentional filtering and selection, allowing us to focus on specific aspects of our environment while ignoring or suppressing others.

While this attentional selectivity is crucial for effective functioning and decision-making, it also means that our perception of the world is always partial and incomplete. We may fail to notice important details or events that fall outside the scope of our attentional focus, leading to gaps and blind spots in our knowledge and understanding. The well-known phenomenon of change blindness, in which people fail to detect significant changes in visual scenes when their attention is diverted, illustrates the powerful role of selective attention in shaping our conscious experience.

Moreover, our cognitive processes are subject to various biases and heuristics that can distort our judgments and beliefs. The confirmation bias, for example, refers to the tendency to seek out and interpret information in ways that confirm our preexisting beliefs and hypotheses, while disregarding or downplaying evidence that contradicts them. This bias can lead us to form echo chambers of self-reinforcing views, and to resist changing our minds in the face of contradictory evidence.

Other cognitive biases, such as the availability heuristic (judging the likelihood of events based on their ease of recall) and the anchoring effect (relying too heavily on the first piece of information encountered when making decisions), further illustrate the ways in which our mental processes can lead us astray and limit the accuracy and reliability of our knowledge.

The limitations of human cognition also extend to the realm of memory, which plays a crucial role in the acquisition, storage, and retrieval of knowledge. While our memories are capable of incredible feats of retention and recall, they are also prone to various errors, distortions, and failures. The phenomenon of false memories, in which people confidently remember events or details that never actually occurred, highlights the constructive and malleable nature of human memory.

Moreover, our memories are subject to various biases and influences, such as the self-serving bias (the tendency to remember events in a way that enhances our self-image) and the hindsight bias (the tendency to see past events as more predictable than they actually were). These biases can lead us to form distorted or inaccurate representations of the past, which in turn can shape our beliefs, decisions, and actions in the present.

The limitations of human cognition also manifest in the realm of reasoning and problem-solving. While our minds are capable of incredible feats of logic, creativity, and insight, they are also prone to various errors and fallacies. The formal fallacies of deductive reasoning, such as affirming the consequent or denying the antecedent, illustrate the ways in which our logical inferences can go awry, even when the premises seem valid and the argument structure appears sound.

Similarly, our problem-solving abilities are subject to various cognitive constraints and biases. The functional fixedness bias, for example, refers to the tendency to perceive objects or concepts only in terms of their usual or conventional functions, making it difficult to find novel or creative solutions to problems. The mental set bias, in which we become stuck in a particular way of thinking or approaching a problem, can likewise hinder our ability to find optimal or innovative solutions.

These cognitive limitations have profound implications for the nature and scope of human knowledge. They remind us that our understanding of the world is not only filtered through the lens of our sensory capacities but also actively constructed and shaped by the particular workings of our minds.

Our mental representations and conceptual frameworks are not perfect mirrors of reality, but rather imperfect and incomplete approximations that are subject to various biases, distortions, and constraints.

Moreover, the limitations of human cognition raise deep questions about the very nature of knowledge itself. What does it mean to know something, if our understanding is always partial, provisional, and subject to revision? How can we adjudicate between competing claims or interpretations, when our cognitive processes are themselves prone to error and bias? These are the kinds of epistemological puzzles that have occupied philosophers and thinkers for centuries, and that continue to challenge our assumptions about the foundations and limits of human understanding.

Recognizing the limitations of human cognition is not a cause for despair or nihilism, but rather an invitation to humility, curiosity, and ongoing inquiry. By acknowledging the constraints and biases that shape our mental processes, we can develop strategies and practices for mitigating their effects and expanding the boundaries of our understanding. This may involve cultivating mindfulness and self-awareness, seeking out diverse perspectives and sources of information, and engaging in critical reflection and self-correction.

Moreover, by recognizing the inherent limitations of our individual minds, we can appreciate the vital importance of collaboration, dialogue, and collective intelligence. By pooling our knowledge, perspectives, and expertise, we can compensate for our individual blind spots and biases, and achieve insights and innovations that would be impossible for any single mind alone.

CHAPTER 39
NEUROLOGICAL COGNITIVE LIMITATIONS

In the previous chapter, we explored the various ways in which human cognition is constrained by the specific sensory, perceptual, and cognitive capacities of the human mind. We discussed how these limitations shape and restrict the scope of what we can know and understand, and how they raise deep questions about the nature of knowledge itself. This chapter delves deeper into the neurological underpinnings of these cognitive limitations, drawing on recent findings from neuroscience and cognitive psychology.

At the core of our discussion is a fundamental insight into the nature of human cognition: adults can typically retain only about four items "in mind" at any given time. This severe limitation in cognitive capacity has been well-documented in psychological literature and is highly correlated with measures of intelligence and cognitive performance. Moreover, reductions in cognitive capacity have been linked to various neuropsychiatric diseases, suggesting a strong biological basis for these limitations.

Recent research in neuroscience has begun to illuminate the neural mechanisms underlying these capacity limitations. Groundbreaking experiments involving the simultaneous recording of neural activity from the parietal and frontal cortices of monkeys performing a visual working memory task have revealed that capacity limitations in visual working memory occur immediately upon stimulus encoding and in a bottom-up manner. This suggests that these limitations are a fundamental feature of how information is processed in the brain.

One key finding from this research is that visual working memory appears to be organized according to a dual model. The left and right halves of visual space were found to have independent capacities, suggesting they constitute discrete resources for information processing. However, within each hemifield, neural information about successfully remembered objects was reduced by the addition of further objects. This indicates that within each discrete resource, there is a limited pool of neural information that must be divided among the objects being remembered. As more objects are added, the amount of neural information available for each object decreases, leading to a decline in the fidelity and robustness of the memory representation.

These findings have significant implications for our understanding of the nature and limitations of human cognition. They suggest that the capacity limitations observed in behavioral studies are not merely a reflection of attentional or strategic factors but are instead a direct consequence of how information is encoded and maintained in the brain. The discrete, slot-like nature of visual working memory resources, combined with the limited pool of neural information within each resource, imposes a hard constraint on the amount of information that can be simultaneously processed and maintained.

Moreover, these neurological constraints may help explain why cognitive capacity is so strongly correlated with measures of intelligence and why reductions in capacity are associated with various neuropsychiatric conditions. If the ability to process and maintain information in working memory is a fundamental building block of higher-level cognitive abilities, then variations in the efficiency and capacity of these neural systems could have far-reaching implications for overall cognitive performance.

The neurological underpinnings of cognitive limitations also raise important questions about the potential and limitations of artificial intelligence (AI) systems. If human-like intelligence is ultimately constrained by the specific architecture and capacity limitations of the human brain, then AI systems that aim to match or surpass human performance may need to grapple with similar constraints. On the other hand, the modular and discrete nature of neural information processing suggests that there may be opportunities for AI systems to overcome some of the limitations of human cognition by employing alternative architectures and processing strategies.

As we continue to explore the neurological basis of cognitive limitations, it is important to keep in mind that our current understanding is still incomplete and subject to revision. The experiments described in this chapter provide a valuable window into the neural mechanisms underlying capacity limitations in visual working memory, but they also raise many new questions and avenues for further research.

For example, how do these capacity limitations relate to other aspects of cognitive processing, such as attention, perception, and long-term memory? How do individual differences in neural architecture and efficiency contribute to variations in cognitive performance? And how can we use insights from neuroscience to design more effective interventions and therapies for individuals with neuropsychiatric conditions that impact cognitive capacity?

As we grapple with these questions, it is clear that the study of cognitive limitations is not just an academic exercise, but a vital area of research with profound implications for our understanding of the human mind and brain. By integrating insights from neuroscience, cognitive psychology, and computer science, we can begin to build a more comprehensive and nuanced picture of the mechanisms and constraints that shape human cognition.

Ultimately, the neurological underpinnings of cognitive limitations remind us that the human mind, for all its remarkable abilities and achievements, is fundamentally a product of the physical brain. As we continue to push the boundaries of what is known and knowable, it is essential that we remain grounded in a deep appreciation for the biological and neurological factors that shape and constrain our cognitive capacities.

CHAPTER 40
LIMITATIONS OF WORKING MEMORY

The human brain is a marvel of cognitive prowess, capable of complex reasoning, creative problem-solving, and abstract thinking. However, despite the remarkable power and flexibility of human cognition, our working memory—the "online" workspace that most cognitive mechanisms depend upon—is surprisingly limited. Studies have shown that an average adult human has the capacity to retain only four items at a given time (1–3). This limitation is not a mere cognitive quirk; rather, it is a fundamental aspect of our cognition that has far-reaching implications for our intellectual abilities and mental health.

Individual variability in working memory capacity is highly correlated with fluid intelligence (4–6), which is the ability to reason and solve novel problems independently of acquired knowledge. In other words, individuals with higher working memory capacities tend to perform better on tasks that require quick thinking, pattern recognition, and abstract reasoning. Conversely, patients with neuropsychiatric disorders often have a reduced working memory capacity (7, 8), which can severely impact their cognitive functioning and quality of life.

Given the central role of working memory in cognition, it is not surprising that capacity limitations have been extensively studied in humans (9). In particular, researchers have focused on the capacity limitation of visual short-term working memory (for reviews see refs. 1 and 4), as vision is the dominant sensory modality in humans and plays a crucial role in many cognitive tasks.

This line of research has led to several competing theories about the neural basis of capacity limitations. "Discrete" models propose that capacity limitations reflect a limit in the number of objects that can be simultaneously represented in working memory (3, 10, 11). According to these models, the brain can only maintain a fixed number of object representations, regardless of their complexity or the amount of information they contain.

On the other hand, "flexible resource" models suggest that only the total amount of information available in working memory is limited, and that this information can be flexibly divided among all represented objects (12–14). Under this view, the brain can store more simple objects or fewer complex objects, depending on the demands of the task at hand.

Another open question in the field is whether the limitation in working memory capacity arises during stimulus encoding or maintenance (15). In other words, is the bottleneck in our ability to initially perceive and store information, or in our ability to keep that information "online" and accessible for ongoing cognitive processes?

To better understand the neural basis of capacity limitations, researchers have turned to animal models, which allow for more invasive and detailed studies of brain activity. In a landmark study, scientists simultaneously recorded from single neurons in the prefrontal and parietal cortex of two monkeys trained to perform a typical human test of cognitive capacity: change localization (Fig. 1A).

In this task, the monkeys were presented with two arrays of colored squares, separated by a short memory delay. In the second array, the color of a randomly chosen square (the target) was changed. The monkeys' task was to detect this change and make an eye movement (saccade) to the target square. By varying the number of squares in the arrays from two to five, the researchers were able to manipulate the cognitive load and study how neural activity changed as a function of working memory demand.

The researchers focused their recordings on three key brain areas: the lateral prefrontal cortex (LPFC), the frontal eye fields (FEF), and the lateral intraparietal area (LIP). These regions were chosen because previous studies had shown that they are critical for short-term memory (16–19) and because human neuroimaging studies had implicated them in capacity limitations (20–22).

By simultaneously recording from multiple electrodes in these areas, the researchers were able to monitor the activity of hundreds of individual neurons while the monkeys performed the change localization task. This allowed them to directly observe how neural representations of the memorized squares changed as a function of cognitive load, and to test the predictions of different models of capacity limitation.

The results of this study provided important new insights into the neural basis of working memory capacity limitations. The researchers found that capacity limitations were evident in all three brain regions, but that they emerged at different stages of the task. In the prefrontal cortex, capacity limitations were already apparent during the initial encoding of the stimulus array, whereas in the parietal cortex, they emerged later, during the memory delay period.

Moreover, the researchers found evidence for both discrete and flexible resource models of capacity limitation. In the prefrontal cortex, neural activity patterns were consistent with a discrete limit on the number of objects that could be simultaneously represented. In contrast, in the parietal cortex, activity patterns were more consistent with a flexible resource model, in which information was divided among all represented objects.

These findings suggest that working memory capacity limitations arise from a complex interplay of discrete and flexible neural constraints, distributed across multiple brain regions and stages of cognitive processing. They also highlight the power of animal models and single-neuron recordings for studying the neural basis of cognitive phenomena that are difficult to investigate in humans.

Of course, much work remains to be done to fully understand the neural mechanisms of working memory capacity limitations. Future studies will need to investigate how these limitations arise from the interactions between different brain regions, how they are influenced by factors such as attention and motivation, and how they relate to other aspects of cognitive function.

Nevertheless, the study described in this chapter represents a major step forward in our understanding of the biological basis of one of the most fundamental and mysterious aspects of human cognition. By revealing the neural circuits and computations that give rise to working memory capacity limitations, this work brings us closer to a mechanistic understanding of how the brain enables the remarkable cognitive feats that define the human experience.

CHAPTER 41
NEURAL MECHANISMS UNDERLYING LIMITATIONS

The previous chapter provided compelling evidence for the existence of capacity limitations in working memory, both at the behavioral and neural levels. Monkeys performing a change localization task showed a decrease in performance as the number of objects in the stimulus array increased, with their information capacity saturating at around four objects. Interestingly, this overall capacity was found to be composed of two smaller, independent capacities for the left and right visual hemifields, each limited to approximately two objects.

These behavioral findings were mirrored in the neural activity recorded from the lateral prefrontal cortex (LPFC), frontal eye fields (FEF), and lateral intraparietal area (LIP). Object information in these areas decreased with the addition of objects to the same hemifield as the encoded object, but not with the addition of objects to the opposite hemifield. This result suggests that the capacity limitations observed in behavior arise from independent constraints on the neural representation of objects in each hemisphere.

The timing of information loss in these areas provided insights into the nature of the capacity bottleneck. When the number of objects exceeded the animals' capacity, information loss began shortly after the onset of the stimulus array and occurred first in LIP, followed by LPFC and then FEF. This bottom-up progression suggests that capacity limitations reflect a failure to perceptually encode objects, rather than a failure to maintain them in memory.

But what is the neural mechanism underlying this encoding bottleneck? Two main hypotheses have been proposed to explain capacity limitations in working memory. The first, known as the "slot" model, posits that objects compete for representation within a limited number of discrete slots, with each object being either successfully encoded or lost entirely (3, 10, 11). The second, the "resource" model, proposes that a limited pool of information is flexibly divided among objects, such that adding more objects reduces the information available for each encoded item (12–14).

The behavioral and neural data from the change localization task provide some support for both models. On a coarse scale, the two hemifields appear to act like separate slots, each with its own independent capacity. However, within each hemifield, the encoding of objects seems to be more graded and resource-like.

When a target object was successfully encoded and the animal correctly detected a change, the amount of information about that specific object in LIP, LPFC, and FEF was still reduced when another object was added to the same hemifield. This finding is inconsistent with a pure slot-like model, which predicts that successfully remembered objects should be represented with equal fidelity regardless of the number of other items in the array.

Moreover, when the animal failed to detect a change to an object, information about that object was not entirely absent from neural activity. LPFC neurons still carried significant information about the missed object during the sample array presentation, although this information was significantly reduced compared to correct trials and continued to decline into the memory delay period. This graded loss of information is more compatible with a resource model, in which the quality of object representations varies continuously depending on the number of items competing for limited neural resources.

These results suggest that working memory capacity limitations may arise from a hybrid of slot-like and resource-like constraints. At a global level, the two hemispheres appear to function as discrete slots, each with its own independent capacity. But within each hemisphere, neural resources seem to be flexibly allocated among objects, with the addition of more items leading to a graded degradation of information about each encoded object.

This hybrid model can account for several key features of the behavioral and neural data. The existence of separate capacities for each hemifield explains why adding objects to the opposite side of the target had no effect on performance or neural information. The resource-like allocation of information within each hemifield explains why successfully encoded objects still suffered a loss of information when other items were added to the same side, and why missed objects were not completely absent from neural activity.

The findings also shed light on the nature of the capacity bottleneck. The early and bottom-up progression of information loss, beginning in LIP and propagating to LPFC and FEF, suggests that capacity limits arise at the stage of perceptual encoding rather than memory maintenance. This observation is consistent with previous theoretical and empirical work pointing to perception as a key bottleneck in working memory (15, 23).

However, the results do not rule out the possibility of additional capacity limits at later stages of processing. The further reduction of information in LPFC late in the memory delay for three-object arrays compared to two-object arrays hints at a potential second bottleneck in memory maintenance. This late-stage limit may reflect the loss of an additional, capacity-independent source of information, such as iconic memory (2), that is available during stimulus presentation but fades during the delay.

The neural mechanisms revealed by this study have important implications for our understanding of working memory and its capacity limits. They suggest that the brain employs a combination of slot-like and resource-like strategies to manage the trade-off between the number of items that can be stored and the fidelity with which they are represented. The division of capacity between the two hemispheres may reflect an adaptive strategy to optimize the allocation of neural resources, while the graded distribution of information within each hemifield allows for a more flexible and efficient encoding of objects.

These findings also have broader implications for the development of artificial intelligence systems that aim to match or exceed human cognitive abilities. The capacity limits observed in biological working memory highlight the importance of designing artificial systems with efficient memory management and resource allocation strategies. The hybrid slot-resource model suggested by this study may provide a useful framework for implementing such strategies in neural networks and other machine learning architectures.

Furthermore, the evidence for a perceptual encoding bottleneck underscores the need for artificial systems to have robust and efficient mechanisms for processing and filtering sensory input. Just as the primate brain appears to be constrained by limits in its ability to encode multiple objects simultaneously, artificial systems may benefit from incorporating attention-like mechanisms that prioritize the processing of task-relevant information.

In conclusion, the study of capacity limitations in primate working memory has revealed a complex interplay of slot-like and resource-like constraints, operating at multiple levels of neural organization. These constraints appear to arise primarily at the stage of perceptual encoding, with a potential secondary bottleneck in memory maintenance. By shedding light on the neural mechanisms underlying these limitations, this research provides valuable insights into the nature of working memory and highlights key considerations for the development of artificial cognitive systems. As we continue to explore the frontiers of biological and artificial intelligence, these findings will undoubtedly inform and inspire new approaches to the design and optimization of information processing systems.

CHAPTER 42
SENSORY ENCODING AND HEMIFIELD INDEPENDENCE

The study of capacity limitations in primate working memory has yielded three key findings that shed light on the neural mechanisms underlying these constraints. First, capacity limits appear to arise during the initial sensory encoding of information, rather than as a failure of memory maintenance. When the number of objects in the stimulus array exceeded the animals' capacity, information loss occurred during the early neural response to the stimulus and was observed first in parietal cortex before propagating to frontal areas. This result aligns with previous work suggesting that an individual's ability to filter information through attention is a critical determinant of their effective working memory capacity (15, 23).

The second main finding reveals the existence of two independent capacities for the left and right halves of visual space. This hemifield independence is consistent with the observation that the capacity bottleneck originates in posterior cortical areas, where neural receptive fields are more tightly confined to a single hemifield compared to those in prefrontal cortex. While human studies have reported varying degrees of hemifield independence (24–27), the strongest evidence comes from divided-attention tasks such as multiple-object tracking (28, 29), which share similarities with the change localization paradigm used in the present study. The requirement to spatially localize the changed object in this task may place greater emphasis on the independence of the two hemifields.

The third key result addresses the ongoing debate between discrete-resource and flexible-resource models of working memory capacity. Discrete-resource models propose that capacity is determined by a limited number of slot-like, independent resources (3, 10, 11), while flexible-resource models suggest a single pool of resources that can be continuously divided among items (12–14). The findings of this study indicate that both mechanisms may be at play, with the two hemifields acting as discrete resource slots, and neural information within each hemifield being flexibly shared among objects in a graded manner. This hybrid model is supported by human psychophysical experiments that demonstrate graded information allocation within discrete slots (30, 31), as well as neurophysiological observations of information multiplexing among prefrontal neurons during the simultaneous representation of multiple objects (32, 33).

The graded loss of information observed within each hemifield raises the intriguing possibility that the underlying neural mechanism may be similar to the competition that occurs during inattention (34–36), even though the animals in this study were actively attending to and remembering all stimuli. The relative independence of contralateral stimuli at the neural level (Fig. 2D) suggests that this competition may be occurring within contralaterally biased receptive fields, which are present even in the lateral prefrontal cortex (18, 37).

An interesting observation that emerges from this study is the apparent difference in capacity limitations between parietal and frontal regions. Parietal neurons seem to be more severely constrained by capacity limits, as evidenced by the lack of above-capacity responses until after the activation of frontal cortex. This finding hints at the possibility that top-down influences from frontal areas may be necessary to partially overcome capacity limits in parietal cortex. It also implies that information must be reaching prefrontal cortex through pathways other than the parietal route, with the ventral visual stream being an obvious candidate. Further experiments will be needed to fully characterize the dynamics of capacity limitations throughout the visual system and to elucidate the role of top-down feedback in modulating these constraints.

The neural mechanisms revealed by this study have important implications for our understanding of working memory and its capacity limits. The evidence for a sensory encoding bottleneck highlights the critical role of attention and perceptual processing in determining the effective capacity of working memory. The independence of the two hemifields suggests that capacity limitations may be tied to the spatial organization of neural receptive fields and the degree of lateralization in the visual system. Finally, the coexistence of discrete and flexible resource allocation strategies points to a hybrid model of capacity that combines slot-like and graded constraints on the neural representation of information.

These findings also have broader implications for the development of artificial intelligence systems that aim to replicate or surpass human cognitive abilities. The capacity limits observed in biological working memory underscore the importance of incorporating efficient attention and encoding mechanisms in artificial systems, as well as the potential benefits of lateralized or modular architectures that can independently process and store information from different parts of the visual field. The hybrid discrete-flexible resource allocation model suggested by this study may provide a useful framework for optimizing the trade-off between the number of items that can be represented and the fidelity of those representations in artificial neural networks and other machine learning architectures.

The study of capacity limitations in primate working memory has revealed a complex interplay of neural mechanisms operating at multiple levels of the visual hierarchy. The sensory encoding bottleneck, hemifield independence, and hybrid resource allocation strategies observed in this study provide valuable insights into the nature of working memory constraints and their neural underpinnings. As we continue to explore the frontiers of biological and artificial intelligence, these findings will undoubtedly inform and inspire new approaches to the design and optimization of information processing systems that can efficiently represent and manipulate multiple objects in a complex visual world.

CHAPTER 43
EXPERIMENTAL DESIGN AND ANALYSIS METHODS

To investigate the neural mechanisms underlying capacity limitations in working memory, the researchers conducted simultaneous recordings from single neurons in the prefrontal cortex (lateral prefrontal cortex, LPFC; frontal eye fields, FEF) and the parietal cortex (lateral intraparietal area, LIP) of two adult rhesus monkeys (Macaca mulatta). The animals were trained to perform a change localization task, which allowed the researchers to manipulate the number of objects in the stimulus array and examine the effects on behavioral performance and neural activity.

In the change localization task (Fig. 1A), each trial began with a short fixation period (500 ms), followed by the presentation of a sample array of colored squares for 800 ms. The relatively long sample period ensured that the animals had sufficient time to attend to and process all items in the array. After a memory delay ranging from 800 to 1,000 ms, a second array was presented, identical to the sample array except for a color change in a single randomly chosen object (the target). The monkeys were rewarded for making a single, direct saccade to the changed object. The stimulus locations were varied daily, with six new locations chosen each day, spanning ±75 angular degrees from the horizontal meridian and between 4° and 6° of visual angle from the fixation point. The colored square stimuli measured 1° of visual angle on each side, and two colors were randomly assigned to each location every day to prevent the monkeys from adopting long-term memorization strategies. Eye position was monitored at 240 Hz using an infrared-based eye-tracking system (ISCAN), and the Monkeylogic program (www.monkeylogic.net) (38, 39) was used for behavioral control of the paradigm.

Simultaneous recordings were made from single neurons in LPFC (584 neurons), FEF (325 neurons), and LIP (284 neurons) using epoxy-coated tungsten electrodes (FHC). The electrodes were lowered into the brain using a custom-built microdrive assembly with 1-mm spacing. All experimental procedures followed the guidelines of the Massachusetts Institute of Technology Committee on Animal Care and the National Institutes of Health.

To estimate the animals' behavioral capacity, the researchers employed an information-theoretic approach that accounted for chance performance and made no assumptions about the animals' strategies in solving the task. First, the information each animal had about each display was determined from its behavioral performance (see SI Materials and Methods for details). By combining this information across displays with the same total number of objects, the researchers could estimate the animals' overall capacity (Fig. 1C). To determine the information capacity in each hemifield, the total information in a given array was decomposed into the information for each hemifield's display (SI Materials and Methods). This hemifield-specific information was then combined for displays of a given size to estimate the animals' capacity in each hemifield (Fig. 2C).

The researchers quantified the information each neuron's firing rate carried about the identity (color) of each object in the hemifield contralateral to the recorded hemisphere using a bias-corrected percentage of explained variance (ωPEV) statistic (Fig. S2 and SI Materials and Methods). To ensure an unbiased analysis, all well-isolated neurons were recorded, and no a priori assumptions were made about the structure of color or location information in neural activity across time or display conditions. The study reports on all neurons that showed significant object selectivity to any stimulus in the sample array (68 neurons in LIP, 189 neurons in LPFC, and 97 neurons in FEF). Neural information was averaged across all selective neurons and all attempted trials, unless otherwise specified (e.g., for correct or error-only trials, Fig. 4).

Two key latencies were of interest in the analysis: (1) when neurons first encoded information about a stimulus, and (2) when this information was degraded due to capacity limitations. To determine the first latency, the researchers asked when the amount of information in a neuron population significantly exceeded baseline. For the second latency, they identified the time point when there was a significant difference in neural information between below- and above-capacity conditions (e.g., one vs. two objects). In both cases, the latency was defined as the time point of maximum rise in the difference function. This maximum rise statistic was used because it is resistant to differences in statistical power; varying the number of neurons in a population will change the threshold of significance but will not a priori affect the shape of the function or the point of maximum slope. The search for the point of maximum rise was limited to a 150-ms window around the first time a significant difference was found (e.g., 191 ms in LIP for greater information in below-capacity trials compared to above-capacity trials). The uncertainty in the time to significance was determined by bootstrapping the population of neurons and re-determining the point of maximum slope.

The experimental design and analysis methods employed in this study allowed the researchers to investigate the neural mechanisms underlying capacity limitations in working memory with high temporal and spatial resolution. By simultaneously recording from multiple brain areas and manipulating the number of objects in the stimulus array, the researchers could examine the effects of increasing cognitive load on behavioral performance and neural activity. The use of an information-theoretic approach to estimate behavioral capacity and neural information ensured that the results were unbiased and accounted for chance performance. The focus on key latencies, such as the onset of stimulus encoding and the timing of information loss due to capacity limitations, provided insights into the temporal dynamics of the underlying neural processes. Overall, the experimental design and analysis methods were well-suited to address the central questions of the study and yielded valuable insights into the neural basis of working memory capacity limitations.